MW01291140

CLARITY

A 30 Day Foolproof Plan for Increasing Your
Performance, Productivity, and Profit

CLARITY

A 30 Day Foolproof Plan for Increasing Your
Performance, Productivity, and Profit

Bob Bohlen & Terry Martin

Copyright © 2010 Bob Bohlen and Terry Martin

Printed in the United States

All Rights Reserved. No part of this book may be reproduced in any form or by any means without prior written permission from the author or publisher except for brief quotations embodied in critical essay, article, or review. These articles and/or views must state the correct title and contributing author of this book by name.

Published by:
Prime Concepts Group Publishing
1807 S. Eisenhower St.
Wichita, KS 67209-2810 USA

Bohlen, Bob.
    Clarity : 30 day foolproof plan for increasing your performance, productivity, profit / by Bob Bohlen and Terry Martin.
        p. cm.
    LCCN 2010932897
    ISBN-13: 978-0-9673164-1-3
    ISBN-10: 0-9673164-1-3

    1. Success in business.   I. Martin, Terry (Terrance) II. Title.

HF5386.B64 2010   650.1
                                QBI10-600150

Dedicated to my wife Lillian.
Thanks for being my best friend and supporter,
and one of America's very best real estate brokers.
Without you, this book would never have happened.

Robert Bohlen

 A Graduate in animal science from the University of Illinois, he soared to the top of the purebred cattle breeding business and worked to provide embryo transfer, embryo freezing and sexing through his sponsorship of veterinarians in this field. He bred and produced numerous national and international champions in several breeds of beef cattle. He also judged at most of the major beef cattle shows in the USA and Canada.

Bohlen was also instrumental in developing the certified Angus Beef Program now featured in many of America's leading restaurants and grocery stores. He was a founder and principal of Premier Beef, Premier Corp, and Premier Angus. These entities were involved in cattle ranching, breeding, feedlot and meat packing operations located in 18 states. He later headed companies in the Coal Mining, Finance, Document Destruction, Real Estate Brokerage, Residential Construction, Interior Design, Title Insurance, and Property Mortgage fields. Bohlen was the number one out of 39,000 real estate agents in the world for Prudential Real Estate 10 out of the 11 years he was associated with them based on total commission income. His firm, Preview Properties, was consistently in the Top 5 single offices with Prudential out of 1600 offices. His firm was based in a town of 5500 residents in Brighton, Michigan.

Bohlen continues to practice Real Estate Brokerage with his wife, Lillian Montalto. Together they own Signature Properties in Andover, MA. Bohlen is also the principal shareholder with a portfolio of 2000 residential apartments and approx 15,000,000 square feet of office warehouse and retail space, which his management company, Anyi Management, manages and operates.

Terry Martin

Terry Martin was born in 1947 in Melbourne, Australia. His early career was in the theater when he travelled the world as stage manager for ballet companies such as the Royal Ballet, National Ballet of Canada and the Australian Ballet. During this time he worked in many of the major theaters of the world, accumulating an unmatched record of international theatrical experience. In 1980 he returned to Australia after 13 years' absence to establish a school for theater technicians. A chance encounter with a wood lathe led to a mid-life change of career as a woodturner and eventually as a wood artist. Martin started writing about the newly developing field of wood art in 1992, combining a lifelong love of photography and writing with his new career working in wood. Today Martin has an unmatched record of publications in the field: over 200 articles in art and woodworking journals, nine years as an editor of a journal devoted to wood art, three books on the field and numerous catalog essays. He is much in demand as a keynote speaker at conferences and symposiums and continues his parallel work as both a creative artist and commentator.

Martin first met Robert Bohlen in 1996, initially when Bohlen started to acquire pieces from him, but later as a contributing writer to the several books Bob and his wife Lillian have published on their art collections. Martin's work is held by significant art institutions throughout the world and particularly in the United States, often courtesy of generous patronage and support from Robert Bohlen. Their relationship has grown into a firm friendship and they continue to share a love of the art that brought them together. In 2008 Bohlen and Terry started to collaborate on this book, a rare example of just how much a friendship and working relationship can evolve.

Foreword

It has been 50+ years since Herman Purdy and J.B. McCorkle showed me a path rarely traveled. Then it was on to Carlo Paterno who hired a mid-western young man to run and manage his east coast operations. It was through him that I had the opportunity to meet and spend time with the likes of J.C. Penney, Eddie Marcus, President Eisenhower, President Johnson, Admiral Strauss, Senator Albert Gore and his wife Pauline, Jimmy Cagney, Jimmy Stewart, Senator Bob Kerr, King Merritt, Paul Benshoof, Allan Ryan, Wally Watts, the Leachman Brothers, Jim Lee Howell, Wilbur May, and many other great business, political and sports minds.

That experience lead me to Bill Brittian who became a great mentor in my early formative years and who challenged me every minute of every hour I spent with him.

As I migrated out of the corporate world into the world of real estate, Mike Ferry and Fred Grosse were great teachers, especially Mike who is the only international trainer I know who really understood the brokerage business as it had to be operated to survive. In addition I have always believed Mike is one of the world's best communicators. He taught a lot about the direct no nonsense method of communication.

To my long term assistants, Regina Benson and Jennie Stuedle, we have closed so many deals that it's easy to remember how much fun and how many challenges we have had together. My son Scott and daughter Lisa who have taken over Preview Properties.

Terry Martin and I have spent time getting these thoughts collected and trying to explain some of the most important life lessons I have learned. If you internalize them and take them to heart they will speed your success and save you years without making the same mistakes I had to make before I learned the life lessons this book contains. The book is created for the benefit of sales people and executives at all levels.

Dig in, and change your life success patterns quickly.

Bob Bohlen
Andover, Mass 01810

Contents

Introduction 15

Phase One – Starting Out with the Basics **23**
Day one: Making sure you stay on target 25
Day two: Living your dreams 30
Day three: Let's really change your life! 35
Day four: Some simple first steps 39
Day five: More simple steps 46
Day six: More ways to make your day better 52

Phase Two – Personalizing the Program **57**
Day seven: Daily Accountability works 59
Day eight: Building a positive attitude 68
Day nine: Taking responsibility 73
Day ten: It's all in the mind 77
Day eleven: Looking ahead 83
Day twelve: Taking even more control of your life 88
Day thirteen: Expanding your horizons 93
Day fourteen: Feeling and looking like success 100

Phase Three – Putting the Program into Practice ... **107**
Day fifteen: Getting down to business 109
Day sixteen: Reinforcing the lessons 115
Day seventeen: Hard-hitting advice 120
Day eighteen: Putting your business plan in writing 127
Day nineteen: Taking a long-term view 133
Day twenty: Friends and associates 137

Phase Four – Business Matters **143**

Day twenty one: Getting the business 145

Day twenty two: Focusing even more 150

Day twenty three: Closing the sale 154

Day twenty four: Making sure the client feels good 160

Day twenty five: Selling is about price, price and price . . 165

Day twenty six: Customer Service makes the difference . . 172

Day twenty seven: Using your time productively 180

Phase Five – Taking the Lead **185**

Day twenty eight: Finding team members 187

Day twenty nine: Managing others 194

Day thirty: Coaching 200

Final Thoughts 205

Appendices 209

Introduction

Here's the promise this book offers: you can change the way you live and work. If you follow Bob Bohlen's program you *will realize your dreams.*

Bob's program will start delivering measurable results sooner than you think is possible. He will show you how to put clear and achievable goals in place and, more importantly, he will show you how to monitor your progress to keep yourself on target.

Bob Bohlen has already produced phenomenal results for people around the world through his mentoring and coaching programs. He is uniquely equipped to show you how to achieve unparalleled success, even when times are tough!

Bob Bohlen's life lessons

Bob has distilled his life experiences into a personal list of strategies that he himself applies in everyday life. He teaches his associates and students to apply these strategies to their own lives and careers. For the first time, this book closely examines these strategies, how Bob developed them, and how anybody can change their life by applying them. Bob calls them **Life Lessons** and he is confident that even if you apply *only one of these Lessons consistently*, that action alone will change your life for the better!

How does Bob Bohlen know so much about success?

During more than 50 years as a businessman, as an art collector, and as a mentor and coach, Bob has achieved outstanding success so many times it is hard to accept that it is all the work of one man. In his most recent career as a real estate broker, Bob is often spoken of as the most successful real estate agent in the world. "I don't know about that," says Bob, "but I do know that during their whole career the average real estate agent in the USA will probably list less than fifty properties." Compare this to the fact that Bob has personally closed sales of 9,600 properties in only twenty years. That's almost 200 times the success rate of the average realtor. What's more, the value of those properties exceeds 2 billion dollars! In 2009 the average annual income of real estate agents in the United States was $35,522, yet Bob has earned tens of millions of dollars in commissions.

Aside from his extensive business successes, Bob is also a major art collector and patron of the arts and his personal collection of sculptural art is among the best in the world. Bob has energized the art world by donating collections of art from artists he has sponsored to many major museums. He has also used his business skills to help museums raise hundreds of millions of dollars.

How has Bob been able to achieve such success? He is absolutely clear on this: "The program I've designed works 100% of the time, without fail. It gets people to lose weight, stop smoking, to earn more money – it's usable in any area of life. It'll work for insurance brokers, securities brokers, managers, entrepreneurs, and blue collar workers. If it's administered and followed carefully, it's ridiculously foolproof."

Why does Bob's program work in so many different areas?

It's because Bob has developed his Life Lessons during a lifetime of remarkably diverse and successful enterprises. "I've been involved in owning, managing, constructing, and deconstructing all kinds of companies over my business career," he says. Bob's career has covered farm management, meat packing, feedlot operations, cattle breeding centers, ranching and crop operations, agricultural workouts, real estate brokerage, residential building, interior design, document services, land development, financial planning, property auctions, title services, mortgage finance, and real estate consulting and coaching.

Bob had achieved outstanding success long before he ever earned a cent selling real estate. In 1969 with 2 associates he started a company with a single employee and within a few years he was employing 3,800 workers. Bob steadily built his meat packing, cattle ranching, and feedlot businesses, and at one time his company owned 500,000 brood cows. The company produced or processed about 4% of all the beef that was eaten in the United States and was an early leader in the artificial insemination process, closely followed by the embryo transplant process and cloning. It was, by any standard, a remarkably successful enterprise.

In 1989, Bob sold his business and, in his own words, "made a pile of money." He had achieved what many dream of – early retirement with enough wealth so that he never needed to work again if he didn't want to. However, Bob quickly found out it was not for him. "I'd planned on not working," he explains, "but I became bored in an instant. Like a lot of people, I thought retirement was the American dream, but within a few days I knew it wasn't what I wanted."

Bob decided to convert some of his real estate assets into a new business. "I looked for a project and decided that a farm I owned in Michigan was ready to be converted into a housing development." Typically, Bob found a new challenge in this experience: "During the project I interviewed the five realtors who were supposed to be the best in the area, but I was very disappointed. Frankly, they were terrible. I thought, 'If these are the best people in this business,

I can do better than that blindfolded!' So you can say that I retired into real estate."

After obtaining his Michigan real estate license, Bob immediately started listing properties. By applying his years of experience in efficiency and quality control standards to his new endeavor, quite soon he was setting new benchmarks for the industry. "I became one of the first residential agents in the USA back in the early 90s to earn a million dollars in commissions in a single year. I've been growing ever since."

In 1991 Bob teamed up with the Prudential Real Estate network and was soon setting new records. He quickly became the number-one overall agent in the world for Prudential and maintained that record for 10 out of 11 years. To help you understand what that means, Bob was competing with 39,000 other Prudential agents! It would have been remarkable enough if Bob was working in one of the larger markets, but as he points out, "Our office was in the very small town of Brighton, Michigan, with around 5,000 residents, and I was competing with agents in New York City, Los Angeles, San Francisco and all the other major metropolitan areas."

In 2001 Bob left Prudential and went back to heading up his independent brokerage company called Preview Properties. com. His company continues to outperform others in the field, but Bob insists it is only because they apply his simple formula for success.

Why does Bob want to tell everybody his secrets?

The answer to that question is simple: *Bob doesn't believe there is any great secret.* His success is based on consistently combining and applying these simple ideas to guarantee reliable results. He wants to share his ideas because he is convinced that helping others reach the levels they aspire to will benefit everybody in the long term. Bob believes that his achievements are not only due to how hard he has worked, but also to the fact that he *strictly follows a program he has developed over many years.*

Bob has honed his program by putting it into practice on a daily basis. In his office and at home, working on the phone, dealing directly with clients, on social occasions, and even buying art for the extensive personal collection he and his wife have assembled, Bob never departs from his own program. Bob explains: "I guess you can say these lessons *are who I am.* I've internalized them because I live by all of them. I'm in the same mode 24/7."

Mentoring for success

For the last ten years Bob has found the time to coach and mentor more than 100 top realtors and other business people from around the world. He's also one of the most popular keynote speakers at national and international events focused on sales success. Unlike many top-level coaches, Bob only works part time at mentoring because he believes that to maintain his edge he needs to personally list, sell and manage real estate every day:

"Apart from running many companies, I also do personal production. On top of that, I've put together a half-billion dollar portfolio of real estate. I'm the principal shareholder and my management company, Anyi Management, administers it."

Bob's track record in predicting trends is equally remarkable. He predicted the bursting of the *Dot.com Bubble* in the late 90s, saving many of his associates from devastating losses. Then as early as 2002 Bob was predicting the collapse of the real estate bubble, enabling him to reposition himself in the market so he is now more secure than almost any of his competitors.

"Five years ago when the real estate market was the best it's ever been in the United States, I started talking about bank-owned properties, short sales, and foreclosures. Everybody thought I had lost my mind, but I could see it coming. I said on record many times that if you loan somebody 103% of the purchase price of a house, and if they lose their job because there is a downturn in the economy, they'll walk away from it. They'll do that because they have no investment in it. Had we not totally reinvented ourselves then we wouldn't even be in business today. Around 85% of our closings last year were representing banks and foreclosed property owners as sellers."

Cut 20 years off your learning curve
Bob's message is simple: "I always tell my students they can save 15 to 20 years by accepting the lessons that it took me nearly 70 years to learn. Don't forget, I got my head handed to me on every one of them, sometimes 5, 10, 15 times before I really understood the lesson. These Lessons can save them from making the same mistakes."

How to use this book
This book will take you on a 30-day journey to radically alter the way you see the world you live in and forever change how you relate to others. After setting up a system of Daily Accountability that will guarantee you stay on target, you will be shown how to reflect on your goals, set targets, focus on your planned activities, and assess your progress as you build up expertise. As you apply the Life Lessons they will start to become second nature and the more you internalize them, the easier it will become. As your life improves, the Lessons will

be constantly reinforced to the point where you will wonder how you ever managed without them.

Bob Bohlen's Program works for people at all levels of personal achievement. If you have never tried to take control of your life before, every day will be a revelation to you. If you feel you already have achieved a high level of life skills, don't worry, you will be challenged soon enough as you reach the more advanced Lessons. If you believe you are already applying some of the ideas you will find in this book, that's good news. However, if you take a fresh look at each idea, you may find new ways to use it. You will be given Daily Tasks to lock in what you have learned and the Program will be more successful if you work your way through the book one day at a time.

From Day One you need to create the habit of finding some quiet time towards the end of the day. It will be a time to reflect on what you have achieved, review how you performed that day, then to read another day's Lessons. You will need an iPhone, laptop, pen and paper, or a dedicated notebook. This will be one of the most important tools in your progress to achieve your goals.

This is important: when you have read your daily Lessons and written down how you will apply them the next day, *stop there!* It won't help you to rush ahead and read all of the book at once because each Lesson builds on previous Lessons. If you haven't had a chance to apply them, there will be no foundation for you to build on. There is no hurry as you have your whole life to benefit from the Lessons Bob has learned.

Among the people Bob coaches in the real estate business, Robert Matheson is one of his most enthusiastic supporters. Robert is based in Canberra, Australia, and is himself a multiple award-winning agent with a track record far exceeding what most agents ever dream of. Robert is confident that Bob has made him a better businessman but, as he explains: "He's also made me a much better person at home. He's made me calmer and helped me appreciate what I have. I spend a lot more time looking forward to what my wife and my children want to do, and I want to help them achieve that too."

You too are about to begin a journey that will change your life. Good luck and enjoy!

PHASE ONE

Starting Out with the Basics

DAY ONE
Making sure you stay on target

Most programs that aim to improve how you live your life don't work because there is no way to accurately and honestly assess your progress against defined goals. It's just too easy to cheat or give up. All over the world people have books on their shelves offering programs that they never fully completed, or never even started putting into action. It is vital to make sure you don't waste this opportunity to change your life through the Bohlen Program.

Today you will set up your personal monitoring system to guarantee that you stay on target to learn from every Lesson Bob has to offer. In fact, this is Bob's very first Lesson:

Daily Accountability is the single biggest step towards improving your life and your productivity

"This is absolutely the most important Lesson of all," says Bob. "It requires you to be reportable or accountable to someone. When people are daily accountable, they plan their days properly and the process requires that they prioritize and optimize how they spend their time. Over and over again I've seen people double or triple their productivity even while they were creating much more free time for themselves, just through Daily Accountability. It's all about focus."

....

Either you run the day or the day runs you.
Jim Rohn, business philosopher

....

Bob repeats with absolute conviction: "You *have to* have somebody to be daily accountable to. You **cannot do it by yourself**. It's true for anybody. You have to find somebody who will hold you accountable, or you will not change your behavior. My own coaching students prove this every week. If they've had a great week they can't wait to talk to me, but if they've had a bad week they would love *not* to talk to me. They duck and dive and weave because they don't like to face up to the fact that they have not performed as well as they should have. *That's why it is important to be accountable.*"

One of Bob's closest colleagues, Mark Herman, President of Anyi Management, gives a really simple example of why it is so important to have some kind of reporting process:

"Let's say you want to lose weight, so you join Weight Watchers," he says. "You're engaged and committed, but if you go to meetings for three weeks and nobody else shows up, you'll either stop going or you'll think 'nobody else cares, so I'll just cheat a little bit.' Unless somebody else is involved, you'll slowly drift away from it. Imagine you're 20 pounds overweight and you have a bad health report from your doctor. He might say 'all you've got to do is walk a mile two or three times a week and that'll take care of a lot of your health problems.' You say 'great,' but if you do it alone and nobody is asking how you are doing, there's no pain in staying in bed one morning. Soon you'll be walking only once a month and not long after you'll quit doing it."

Not surprisingly, Bob also has many examples to offer, including from his own office. "Every agent I coach and every agent in our firm faxes or e-mails me what I call a 'Daily Accountability Form.' It tells me what their day was structured like, and that includes how many calls they made; how many appointments they had; how many appraisals, evaluations, or listing presentations they made; whether they were on track on a scale of 1-10 or not; and what they have to accomplish for the week. Once a week I have them send me their top prospect list. For a sales rep. or agent that means their top buyer and top seller candidates. We set a potential commission income for them. That helps them prioritize who they really need to be spending time with."

Phil Herman, a remarkably successful real estate agent who Bob has coached for many years also confirms what Bob says: "Accountability is the most important thing Bob teaches. I think that when a lot of people first hear the word 'accountability,' it has a negative connotation, but Bob presents it in such a way that it isn't negative. Bob is saying 'Let me introduce you to a tool that can propel you beyond your wildest imagination.'"

On Bob's website where his students post feedback Bryan Barnes from Toronto, Canada, is unequivocal in his support for this idea: "Every time I think about accountability, I wonder where it has been all my life. Real estate is the best business in the world for getting away with doing nothing and not getting caught, because nobody cares! My son has just started with me and as I make him accountable, I find he is already miles ahead of where I was when I started."

Bob sums up the importance of Daily Accountability: "Let's imagine you are phenomenally self-disciplined and you write down your goals with the *maximum degree of specificity* and a clear date for accomplishing those goals. Let's say that you look at that plan three or four times a day. There is no doubt that it will keep you focused and you will be much more likely to accomplish your goals than if you don't write them down and you don't put specific timeframes around them. But you are still only **half as likely** to accomplish them as you are if somebody holds you accountable. It's because we all kid ourselves all the time and we don't do what we say we will do, or we kid ourselves that we are doing it when in fact we are way off track. This way you can't fool yourself."

Of course there may be people who think they don't have access to a suitable mentor. "But it's not true," Bob says. "I believe that e*veryone* looks up to someone in their life. They can ask that person to hold them accountable. If it's appropriate they can pay them, or they can trade something to get that person to hold them accountable. It might be a person who is willing to do it because of a strong personal connection. Sometimes just the idea of disappointing the person they respect is enough to make sure they do what they committed to. It can easily be a relative, like an aunt or a brother, but it has to be somebody they have a great respect for. Even the greatest loner has to talk to other people."

Mark Herman further describes it as follows: "It's finding an individual who will take the process seriously, and will also allocate his or her time and talent to the process on a periodic basis to make sure you remain engaged. If you are not held accountable to maintain the process you are committed to, it won't happen."

It might seem that the mentor will need some special motivation or reward to remain on task, but Bob doesn't think this is a challenge. "It's very simple. If the student shows appreciation for what the mentor is doing and shows that they are committed, that will keep the mentor interested. If the student doesn't show appreciation, or doesn't follow the program, it breaks down and within days or weeks there isn't any relationship. So really it is up to the student, not the mentor."

Finding a mentor

It's time to identify someone to be your guide, so now you need to get out your pen and paper to begin planning.

First, make a list of all the people you can think of who you respect and see on a regular basis. You can include family members such as your parents, in-laws, brothers and sisters, friends' parents, teachers or past teachers, work colleagues, employers, a respected neighbor, a close friend, and so on. Only you will know who is best to ask, but it is important that you start your list now. It would be perfect if they are people you see often, but if that isn't possible, a mentor you can regularly stay in touch with will work. Eventually you are going to refine this list to arrive at the best candidates.

Today's Lesson is so important that it is the first of only two days when you will learn just one Lesson:

> ■ **Daily Accountability is the single biggest step towards increasing and improving your life and your productivity**

Tomorrow's task:

Making your mentor list is your first task under the Bohlen program. It will support everything you do over the next 30 days, so tomorrow you will need to give more thought to potential mentors and add them to your list. Enjoy the task! It's not often we take the time to think of all the people we respect and admire, so you might surprise yourself.

DAY TWO
Living your dreams

Yesterday you were asked to list potential mentors. By now you should have some names, but there is still time to refine the list. Before you finally select your mentor you need to learn about identifying your dreams and converting those dreams into action plans. You need to know where all this is going.

First, ask yourself this simple question:

What would I like to do with my life?

Now, let's make another simple list. Write down some of the big things you dream of achieving in your life. This is a chance for you to let your imagination run free, so *surprise yourself!* Write down at least five things that you believe would make your life more complete. Don't think too hard, just *stop reading now and do it!*

....

Champions aren't made in the gyms.
Champions are made from something they have
deep inside them: a desire, a dream, a vision.
Muhammad Ali

....

Now you have written down your dreams, ask yourself honestly, are any of these dreams part of your life plan? Do you even have a life plan? If not, don't worry. Before you have finished the Bohlen Program you will and your dreams will be the starting point for that life plan. Bob's Lesson is:

Without a dream you will go nowhere

Bob explains: "It's hard for most people to imagine that they could achieve almost anything they want. It's because they get all hung up on the process of going somewhere, rather than focusing on their end point. Most people don't get what they want *because they don't know what they want.*"

For years Bob has been mentoring Rick Ferris, who runs a highly successful real estate enterprise in northeast Ohio. He confirms the importance of what Bob says. Rick believes that everybody's dreams are different and you need to find your own. When he met Bob, Rick's dream was to work less hours and still earn the same income. "I achieved that dream", he says. "Now I only work about thirty hours a week and I take fifteen weeks off each year, but I still make the same amount that I used to make when I was working fifty hours a week. I could earn more if I worked more, but I really like doing everything else! It gave me a focus that I would never have achieved before."

Bob says, "The next step after you have identified your dream is to make it into an actual objective, something *concrete.* That's the difference between a dream and a goal."

Goals have to be in writing or you won't achieve them

Bob's Lesson applies to everything you dream of achieving. "If goals aren't important enough to write down, they aren't very important," he says. "I write down everything I want to do, and that's one of the ways I internalize things. When I write it down, I remember it. Writing it down forces you to go through the thought process in a structured way rather than the scattered way most people think about things. It usually goes something like, 'Maybe I'll do A, or B, or maybe C.....' The result is that they don't know if they want to do one or the other, or even all three! When you write it down, you focus, commit it to paper and know what you are going to do."

Bob has seen this happen so many times that he is convinced it will work for everybody. "Out of all the people I've worked with, and that's thousands, I have seen very few achieve anything they didn't write down. Part of that is the actual exercise of writing it down. It causes them to subconsciously accept that it's more important than all the other things they didn't write down. If you write it down and put it in front of you, then you focus on it. When you focus your energy on things, you get them done."

· ·

The most important thing about motivation
is goal setting. You should always have a goal.
Francie Larrieu Smith,
five-time U.S. Olympic team member

· ·

Bob has a list of personal and business goals that he updates constantly. He says that he invariably accomplishes almost all of them. "How would I be able to do all these things and know what I had accomplished unless I had written them down? It'll work for anybody. What's more, once they start this process, it will give them more confidence that they can achieve whatever they want to."

A lot of people find their work a daily grind and it seems they could never link their dreams with their jobs. In fact most people's dreams probably revolve around escaping work. If they hate their job that's not surprising, but Bob believes if they see that their dreams can become reality, they will not only work harder, but they will enjoy it as well. Dreams can be the strongest motivating force to help people enjoy work more. His Lesson is:

If people don't have something passionate to work for, they won't work

"I've learned over the years," said Bob, "that if people don't have something they are really passionate about to work for, they just show up at work and don't use their time productively. In fact they just spend the time. Of course, the opposite is equally true. If they *do* have something they're passionate about, they'll work harder to achieve it!"

An average person with average talents and ambition and average education, can outstrip the most brilliant genius in our society, if that person has clear, focused goals.
Mary Kay Ash, author *You Can Have It All*

Mark Herman explains further: "Bob is absolutely right. This Lesson is about how your dreams can drive your professional life, but it's also about how success in your professional life can enhance your friendships, your opportunities, or your personal desires outside of work. It's a two-way process. For example, you might be committed to a cancer support charity, or it may be your love of the arts, or travel. Let's say a family member is going through a divorce and he or she is left in a difficult situation, you may be able to provide a rental house for them to help them through the process. You might fund a college education for your siblings, or extended family members like nieces or grandchildren if they can't do it on their own. With these goals in mind, working hard to earn enough to achieve them is that much easier. These are real examples of how I've viewed the lessons and incorporated them into my life."

Today's Lessons show you that dreams are more than just fantasies. They will drive you to achieve all that you want. In fact, you've already taken this step. When you wrote down your dreams at the start of this chapter, you were writing down the first part of your new life plan. These Lessons are the starting point for all of the Lessons you will act on over the next twenty eight days:

- **Without a dream you will go nowhere**
- **Goals have to be in writing or you won't achieve them**
- **If people have something passionate to work for, they'll work harder**

Tomorrows' tasks:

This task is one of the easiest you will do. Reflect on your list of dreams and add to it if you can. They don't all have to be big dreams. These dreams, both large and small, will be the main motivator for you over the coming weeks and months. Take your list of dreams with you tomorrow and when you have time, look at it again. As you read your dream list, keep this in mind: *these dreams are not just an escape from reality. They can become your new reality!* If you follow Bob's program carefully, you will make these dreams come true.

Your second task is to keep thinking about people you know who might understand your dreams and who would like to see you realize them. They are the ones you want to keep on your mentor list!

DAY THREE
Let's really change your life!

Bob believes that one of the reasons people can't make progress with their lives is that they are afraid of change. "Most people fight change in every aspect of their lives," he says. "If you are going to achieve what you are capable of, *you are going to have to change your behavior.* So Bob's Lesson is:

Welcome change, don't fight it

"If you see challenges as opportunities," says Bob, "then one door closes and another opens. You view life more positively and it allows you to excel when other people aren't because they are fighting the change. A lot of people hope that if they don't do anything, everything will stay the same forever. But it won't. I believe that *the minute you are satisfied with where you are, you aren't there any more.* The world is progressing. For example, look at how people communicate these days. They depend so much on the Internet, but fifteen years ago there wasn't any Internet to speak of. We were one of the first real estate firms to be on the Internet in 1995. Now *all* real estate business is on the Internet. These days you have your desktop and laptop, and soon you will be using your iPhone as your computer, if you aren't already. Before we were the gatekeepers of the information because people had to come to us to find it. Now everybody has the information and there is so much out there that they don't know how to relate to it. So now we're the translators of the information. That's the reason we still have a job as real estate agents. We welcomed the change."

If you don't like change,
you're going to like irrelevance even less.
General Eric Shinseki, Chief of Staff, U.S, Army

Again, Rick Ferris confirms that Bob has it right: "When I first heard about Bob's idea of bringing clients into my office instead of me going to them, I thought, 'That might work for Bob, but it will never work for me, not in my market!' Then one day I thought I'd try it with owners who are selling their own properties because they can be really difficult to deal with. I called around thirty just as a test to see if I could get them to come into my office. To my amazement, one out of five agreed to come in! So of course I tried it with my regular clients. For a while I was worried about whether I'd get a 'yes' or a 'no,' but then I realized I just didn't have to take 'no.' So I simply negotiated a time when they could come in. Now I can say that among the 300 other people I am competing with in my market, there is absolutely nobody else who does it. I discovered I didn't have to do what everybody else does. Unless Bob had pushed me to accept new ways, I would never have done it."

To help people overcome their fear of change, when he is coaching much of Bob's energy goes into helping people focus on their objectives and then *committing themselves to achieving them.* His next Lesson clearly states this:

The process for change is:
Awareness, Decision, Commitment

Bob explains: "To change something, you first need to become aware of what you want to change. Many people go through life thinking everything is just fine, but once you are aware that things aren't as good as they could be you need to make an unequivocal decision about what it is you want to change and that you really want to do it. It might be, 'I want to get a college diploma,' or 'I want to generate more income.' That first decision is important, but the decision is irrelevant if you don't make a clear commitment to make the change."

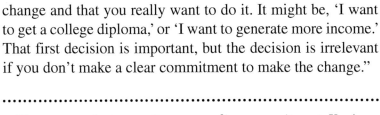

There are only two options regarding commitment. You're either in or out. There's no such thing as a life in-between.

Pat Riley, widely regarded as one of the
greatest NBA coaches of all time

As an example of this, Bob tells the story of a man who worked for him who wanted to lose 100 pounds. "He asked me for help and I agreed. Once he had convinced himself that he really wanted to lose the weight, we discussed how he would do it and when he would achieve it. I held him accountable to his plan and two days before the deadline he weighed in. He had lost the 100 pounds. Not 99, or 101, but *exactly* 100! It wasn't an accident that he lost exactly that amount of weight. It was because he wrote down the target and he did exactly what he needed to do to reach it. He had written it down and committed to it. Also, he had a reward in place to encourage him, and a major non reward that acted as a pitchfork in his behind to move him towards his goal."

You have to commit. I think the biggest word is commit. I hear women say to me all the time, and men – I want to, I want to.

Suzanne Somers, best selling author
and businesswoman

Bob grants that there is more to fully succeeding than just saying you are committed, but he insists that, "At this stage

it's enough to understand that these two Lessons are funda-
mental to changing how you lead your life."

- ▆ **Welcome change, don't fight it**
- ▆ **The process for change is: Awareness, Decision, Commitment**

Tomorrow's tasks:

Tomorrow you need to refer again to your list of dreams from
day two. This time, choose the dreams that mean the most to
you, then *rewrite your list to include only these most important dreams.* Soon you will be shown how to quantify these
dreams and turn them into reality, but for now follow these
three important steps to change how you are thinking:

Awareness: Rewrite your list. By refining your list and choosing the dreams that mean the most to you, you have made
yourself more aware of what matters to you.

Decision: Look at the list again and ask yourself this simple
question. *Do I really want these dreams to come true?*

Commitment: Embrace the idea that these dreams will come
true and commit yourself to the idea that you will do all that
you can to make it happen. Carry this list with you from now
on and refer to it often – it is your primary inspiration.

DAY FOUR
Some simple first steps

So far you've learned about Daily Accountability, turning your dreams into goals, and committing to change. As you continue with the Bohlen plan, you will develop these Lessons further. Over the first two days you made your list of possible mentors as well as your enhanced list of dreams that will become concrete goals. Remember to keep both these lists near you as they will drive all of the Lessons to come.

Bob believes that some of the most effective Lessons are really very easy to understand and to put into action. Today he starts introducing you to some of these simple Lessons and the first is:

What you are doing should be fun every day.
If it isn't, do something else

Bob tells the story about something he and his wife Lillian recently experienced: "We drove into a gas station last week. It was both a self-serve and a full-service station. Even though we were in the self-serve lane, the guy bopped out, washed the window, and said 'Hi! How are ya? How can I help you?'

I said to Lillian, 'He owns the place.' She agreed.

When I got out I asked him and he said 'Absolutely!'

We could tell by his energy that he loved what he was doing and that his success depended on what he did. Sure, it's not exactly the same for an employee, but if the boss is enthusiastic, they're going to enjoy working for him and it's likely to rub off. They're much more likely to enjoy their work and respond to customers in the same way. The most important thing is that if somebody is not enjoying their job, they won't be good at it."

....

If you work just for money, you'll never make it.
But if you love what you are doing, and always
put the customer first, success will be yours.
Ray Kroc, developer of McDonalds

....

"If somebody really doesn't like their job and just can't get enthusiastic, they need to get a new job. They should *just walk away.*" Bob offers this example: "I go to a hotel where about eight months ago the chef hired a really good maitre d.' He was really terrific at his job and trained his staff so they were all many times better than when he arrived. Despite all that, he recently resigned. He said it was because he wasn't having that much fun at it and he didn't want to do it for the rest of his life. Now he has a 9-to-5 job marketing software and he's enjoying it much more."

....

Success is not the key to happiness.
Happiness is the key to success. If you love
what you are doing, you will be successful.
Albert Schweitzer, philosopher and physician

....

"If a person feels they aren't able to walk away, they'll stay unhappy," says Bob. "But if you want to take control of your life, there's no better place to start than with what you do every day. If you find something you enjoy doing, you'll get better and better at it. The better you get, the more you enjoy it, and then you become even better at it! You notice it imme-diately. I believe that if you love doing something the money will follow. Even in this time of high unemployment, employers will always find room in their operations for people who demonstrate a love of what they are doing."

....

I never did a day's work in my life. It was all fun.
Thomas A. Edison

....

Michael Edlen first met Bob fifteen years ago when they were both making a big impression in the real estate industry. They have maintained a steady respect for each other's achievements ever since. Michael supports Bob's idea about enjoying what you do, but he adds: "Of course, for many people it isn't practical to do something else, but I've always found it helpful to remember that it's all in your mental attitude towards what you do each day. I think that almost anyone can find something to enjoy in what they do. It can mean changing the way you think and the way you work. In my earlier life I worked in manufacturing, but because it was a family business it wasn't practical to change my job. It was a difficult exercise for me to find parts of it that I could enjoy, but I did it by challenging myself to do something better than our competitors could."

Anybody who watches Bob at work will see that he enjoys it immensely. "I find sales fun because I enjoy closing transactions and working on the presentations to do that. But I also enjoy seeing people that I work with grow and succeed. When you see people mature and grow and in turn provide leadership for other people, that's really satisfying. On top of that, if you enjoy your professional life, all of the other parts of your life will become easier. Your mood will be better so you and your family will be more at ease. Also, you're likely to be healthier because you will be less stressed. It's also a fact that if you are happy you will work better, earn more and then you can do more of the things you like to do in your free time."

Do you enjoy what you do?

It's time to ask yourself if you really love your job. When you get up in the morning, are you looking forward to your day? If the answer is yes, congratulations! You are ahead of the game! If you are not so sure, let's look at some ways you can make it happen.

Firstly, you are not alone. For many people work is something to be endured and it never occurs to them that they might be able to control this significant part of their lives. So what's the difference between those people and the others who enjoy their work?

Those who don't enjoy their working life often talk about 'getting out of work' or 'escaping.' In contrast, people who enjoy what they do probably enjoy the company of those they work with, have a sense of achievement, and feel their work is meaningful. They feel focused and in control because they know what they have to do and how to do it. You need to gain that sense of purpose and meaning.

••

Don't ask yourself what the world needs; ask yourself what makes you come alive. And then go and do that.
Harold Thurman, African-American author,
educator and civil rights leader

••

Because you spend a significant portion of your life working, don't waste it doing something you hate. Successful people enjoy their work because they see how it fits into their life plan. They see each day's work contributing to the fulfillment of the dreams that we talked about on day two. The good news is that there are strategies you can use to help yourself.

Strategies for a better life

You can start improving your life right now by putting yesterday's experiences behind you and treating every day as a fresh start. Bob's first Life Lesson for tomorrow is:

Start each day at zero

Bob always keeps a lined yellow pad lying on his desk with a hand-written list on it. Every evening he writes his "to do" list on this pad. "I use it to keep track of all the things I wants to do the next day," Bob explains. "It forces me to look at what I accomplish each day, assess the results, and pre-plan the activities for the next day. People ask me if the yellow pad has some significance, but it was just something I started with years ago and I stuck with it." As a talisman, something symbolic to focus his attention on that particular task, it is an effective tool.

"I've found that by using this system, several good things happen. Although I do write down any remaining challenges, I also wipe the slate clean so I don't think about business again until the next day. I sleep better and business doesn't interfere with my personal life. After I get up each morning, shower and eat breakfast, I'm ready to start the new day from zero, uncluttered, prioritized and organized."

••

*The best thing about the future is that
it comes one day at a time.*
Abraham Lincoln

••

Another bonus of this method is that it helps Bob retain control over when he performs each task. "By prioritizing ahead I am able to do the hardest and perhaps most unpleasant task first. It gets it out of the way and I feel better about the rest of the day. That way I get far more accomplished than I would by deferring my challenges until the day's end when I have a lot less energy."

In fact you are already applying this Lesson! When you made your mentor list on day one and listed your dreams on day two, you were already prioritizing your life. You probably didn't use a lined yellow pad, but you might consider selecting a pad or notebook that is different from all your other writing materials. Small symbolic steps like this do have a certain power to help you change the way you live. It has to do with the process of visualizing, recording, and, above all, committing yourself to change, which we talked about yesterday.

Bob is absolutely clear about the effectiveness of this strategy: "It's an amazing thing! Thinking about setting goals in my experience gets no results. Writing them down always seems to help make them happen."

We will be looking at this in more detail later, but for now let's concentrate on this simple act of writing down your plan for the coming day.

Tomorrow's plan:
Think of what you would like to achieve tomorrow. It doesn't have to be at work. Is there a phone call you should make? Do you need to clean out the attic? Does your dog need walking? When you have finished your list some of them might not seem so important any more, so you can cross them off.

If you are going to be at work tomorrow, what can you think of that will make your day more productive, will make others notice you, and leave you with a feeling of achievement? Remember what Bob said and don't put off the hardest task till the end of the day, or you may not get it done at all. Maybe you need to rework your filing system, or you want to get that new printer and set it up at your desk. It might be as simple as improving your output per hour. What you think of doesn't have to be *very* important, but it will be part of the day's achievements. Whatever you write, be realistic and be determined.

At the end of tomorrow you will have the pleasure of going through your list and crossing off all the things you have done. The most important thing is that you will have a sense of achievement. For now you should keep the pages that record your achievements. They will become a tangible record of how you are changing your life and later in the book you will refer back to them.

By the way, after reflecting on your life you may decide that the most important thing you need to do is walk away from your job. Congratulations! You have taken an enormous step towards making the rest of your life a success. If you go ahead with that plan tomorrow, your list of things to do should now include finding a job that you will enjoy.

Let's remind ourselves of today's Lessons:

- **What you are doing should be fun every day. If it isn't, do something else.**
- **Start each day at zero**

Think again on these Lessons and then remember, before you go to bed, **write down the things you want to achieve tomorrow.**

Tomorrow's task:
Work your way through the list of things you want to achieve. While you are doing it, ask yourself this really important question again: *are you really enjoying your job?*

DAY FIVE
More simple steps

Today you completed your first day of working from a to-do list. It doesn't matter if there are still a few unfinished tasks, as long as you tried hard to complete them. You need to learn what you can achieve in a day and there is time to stretch yourself as you become more efficient. Now you need to scratch off each of the completed tasks. It feels good doesn't it?

After you have moved any uncompleted tasks to tomorrow's to-do list, take some time to reflect further on how much you enjoyed your day. Was it more enjoyable when you had a set of targets to accomplish?

Today you are going to learn three more simple Lessons that you can apply right at the beginning of your next working day. The first of these is:

Always be early

Do you tend to arrive late for work or appointments? There's no way around it, *when you are late you leave a bad impression*. Bob not only believes this is important, but he strictly applies this Lesson to himself.

"If I didn't do what I said I'd do on time," says Bob, "how would anybody trust me next time? Remember, the first impression lasts for a long time and the beginning of an appointment is when important impressions are made. It's better not to be late and have to spend the next four or five appointments trying to overcome that bad first impression."

....

Seventy percent of success in life is showing up.
Woody Allen, Academy Award-winning film director

....

"I always try to be early," Bob explained further. "One of my mentors was Bo Schembechler, the great Michigan football coach. He had a great saying: *'Early is on time, on time is late.'* He was right you know. If you're even a little bit late, you send a signal to your appointment that you just don't care. Of course, despite your best preparations, something may happen to make you late. It happens to me, but it's very rare, maybe two or three times a year out of hundreds and hundreds of appointments. If I'm running a few minutes late, I call ten minutes ahead of time, or have my assistant call to advise my appointment. But I see many people consistently showing up late for appointments and the message it sends is that they are inconsiderate and really don't care about the other person's time."

So there's your first challenge for the day. Get to work early! You'll find yourself less stressed because you'll have time for a coffee, time to talk to people you work with, time to *give a good impression.* You can write this on the top of you to-do list: *get up early enough to get to work early.* It can be the first thing you cross off your list. Pretty soon it will become a habit.

While we are talking about making good impressions, let's look at another Life Lesson that will help you do this.

Give out several compliments each day that come from your heart

Bob knows that one of the best ways to leave a good impression on other people is to acknowledge their achievements. The good thing is that it becomes a part of the positive feedback loop. If you make other people feel good about themselves, it's amazing how good it can make you feel about yourself.

I can live for two months on a good compliment.
Mark Twain

"A lesson I learned years ago," says Bob, "is that in many companies it is your receptionist and your truck drivers that represent you most often, because other people might never see you, but they see them. That's why for example, I always let our receptionist know how important she is. I might say, *Wanda, you're so important to the company. We really appreciate the positive energy you create at the front desk.* Another example is Phil, who has been our maintenance man since we started business. He's one of the most important employees we have, so I let him know that I notice. I might compliment somebody else on their appearance by saying something like: *Frank, that's a great suit you have on today.* Mentioning somebody's performance is always appreciated, such as: *Lisa, good job on getting that property on the market and thanks for getting it all processed so quickly.*

"But you have to mean it," Bob cautions. "People can read a phony compliment as fast as you can say it. If you don't mean it, it doesn't mean anything, so make sure you mean every word, and remember, p*eople never forget how you make them feel.*"

When employees are happy,
they are your very best ambassadors.
James Sinegal, co-founder of Costco,
the largest U.S. wholesale club

Mark Herman confirms how important this Lesson is: "Any time you are positive and heartfelt in your feedback, I think it allows you to operate at a much more intimate level with people. Also, I think the element of surprise or unpredictability is very powerful. If you are working very hard and doing a good job, then without warning somebody drops a wonderful compliment on you, whether its written or in person, you can't help be lifted and feel pretty darn motivated by it."

....

*No matter how busy you are, you must
take time to make the other person feel important.*
Mary Kay Ash, founder of Mary Kay Cosmetics

....

Bob has another Lesson on this subject:

You can make more friends in a month by being interested in them than in a lifetime trying to get them interested in you

Try it. It's one of Bob's simplest Lessons and it brings results every day.

While we are on the subject of making people feel good, you might be thinking about how people you work with don't seem to appreciate what you do. You will be surprised how they will notice you more once you start to notice them and acknowledge what they do. It's simple human nature.

When you write your plan for tomorrow, write down today's Life Lessons on a card. You can use it during the day to remind yourself to act on them.

- **Always be early**
- **Give out several compliments each day that come from your heart**

- **You can make more friends in a month by being interested in them than in a lifetime trying to get them interested in you**

Choosing your mentor

We have reached a very important stage in your progress to realizing your dreams. It's time to make a decision about choosing your mentor. By now you have learned enough Lessons that you could be reporting daily progress to a mentor, so it's time to establish that all-important relationship. Tomorrow you need to speak with the person you think will be your best mentor. You should explain the Bohlen plan to them, show them what you have learned so far and ask them if they can commit to helping you. How you negotiate this relationship will depend on your personal circumstances, but **you must do it!** It will help to refer back to Day One to refresh your memory. In fact, this is a good time to review everything you have learned so far and then you will be better equipped to answer any questions your potential mentor might have.

If you explain that you are asking them to do it because you believe they are a positive person and that you respect them very much, that they are smarter than you are and better at what they do than you are, Bob believes that *almost without exception they'll be flattered when you come and talk to them and they'll offer to help you.*

The person you approach will probably ask how much time it will all take. The ideal mentor will be someone you can report to every day, but if they are not available every day you can negotiate a plan that will fit in with their availability. For example, if they are only available once a week, you can arrange to report to them about each day's activities for a one-week period. You may agree with them that they will give you between 5 and 10 minutes every day, but if they are too busy for that, they might accept 15 to 30 minutes once a week. You will learn about this in more detail soon, but for now you should have enough information to approach your choice for mentor.

If the first person you ask is not able to help you, work your way through your list until you get a positive response. Whatever else you do, make sure you present the idea in a positive way. In fact this is an opportunity to put one of today's Lessons into practice. After all, there can be no bigger compliment than to tell someone you respect them enough to ask them to help guide you to a better life!

If you get a positive response, you can also show them your list of dreams. Tonight you may want to refer to that list again and refine it before you show them. That very act will focus your attention more on your dreams and is a foretaste of the experience of being Daily Accountable. After all, it's not every day you share you dreams with someone else.

Good luck and remember how important this is!

"Daily Accountability", says Bob, "is absolutely the *most important Lesson of all.*"

Tomorrow's tasks:
Your first task is to make your to-do list for tomorrow. Don't forget to put today's three Lessons on a card and refer to them often! This is a good strategy for every day's Lessons, so you should add more Lessons to your card every day. Eventually you will internalize them to the point that you don't need to have them on a card, although it will always be important to regularly review even the simplest Lessons to remind yourself of how important they are.

The second task is one of the most important you will complete: *talk to your preferred mentor.*

DAY SIX
More ways to make your day better

Before we begin today's Lessons, your main task today was to talk to your mentor of choice. If they agreed to help you, congratulations! Bob has this advice for you: "At this stage the most important thing is for you to show you appreciate them agreeing to help you. From now you need to explain to them, step-by-step, the program that you will learn over the coming days. Then you must carefully follow that program because if you don't, within a few days or weeks it will break down and there won't be any relationship. I believe the teacher always learns the most and if they are the right person to be a mentor, they'll really appreciate what is happening and stay on track. If they aren't the right person, then it's better to find somebody else anyway."

Today's Lessons also seem very simple, but remember that you are building up an interlocking series of strategies that together will change the way you live.

Bob explains that what people say to each other is not always what it appears: "Most people fib to each other all the time," he says. "That's why when people make statements such as, *'We're the best company in Texas,'* nobody believes them. It's because they don't believe what *they* tell other people. If you puff the facts, the next time you talk to somebody you may not remember what you told them and the facts will be different. It always catches up with you."

So Bob's Lesson is:

Just tell the truth

It seems too simple doesn't it? Well, just ask yourself, do you sometimes exaggerate to impress people? If you do, and most people do, do you think it works in the long term? Next time you are trying to impress somebody, take note of what they say when you are done. It's likely they will try to top what you told them, or they will have already switched off.

> *What people say, what people do, and what they say they do are entirely different things.*
> Margaret Mead, American cultural anthropologist

Mark Herman could not agree more:

Telling the truth is the foundation for everything," he says. "There is no grey area. You either do it or you don't. If you do, you never have to worry about it, but if you don't it'll come back to haunt you."

Robert Matheson, who you met at the start of this book, has no hesitation in agreeing that this simple Lesson is important: "Sometimes we see clients who think their house is worth much more than it really is. Anybody can just agree with them, but it's much harder to tell someone what they need to hear. It can reduce your chance of getting the business when you tell them their home is worth considerably less, but eventually they will see the truth of what you say and that can create a solid relationship for future business. In the process you can save them months of pain and save yourself a lot of time."

Michael Edlen likes to say that telling the truth begins with personal principles. "It starts with being honest with yourself, being principle oriented, and not concerning yourself too much with what other people may choose to do. I think that, deep down, most people do want to know what's true, but you have to be careful because the truth can be unintentionally hurtful. Luckily, experience tells you how and when to tell the truth."

This simple Lesson is supported by Bob's next Lesson:

Generally the simpler something is, the better it is

Bob explains: "All my Lessons are aimed at simplifying life. The old motto is that *the shortest distance between two points is a straight line.* I find it's always true. When you start zigzagging all over the map, you lose direction. Usually it means you've become tied up in the process, not the objective. When people make things complicated, they generally can't make them happen."

Again, Michael Edlen agrees: "Most of the time when a situation seems complicated, it's often because we've made it that way. If we reduce it to the basic elements it makes it far easier to solve. Sometimes when a problem is reduced to it's simple parts, it even resolves itself! The whole situation might have become complicated because somebody started out with one incorrect premise. Once that is fixed, it all falls into place."

Bob makes a surprisingly simple observation to support this Lesson: "I can tell a lot about somebody by looking at their desk. If it's organized and clear, it tells me they are thinking clearly. So if you want to start simplifying your life, a good place to start is right where you work. My rule is:

A cluttered desk creates a cluttered mind

"If you are surrounded by mess," says Bob, "how are you going to organize your thoughts? It doesn't have to be a desk. When you take your car in to be fixed, look into the workshop. You can tell a lot about mechanics by how they look after their tools. Do you really want somebody working on your car if they don't know where a particular wrench is, or if their floor is covered in oil? Anybody can improve their efficiency by cleaning up their workspace and the good news is that it will help them clear up their thought processes as well."

....

Simplicity is a prerequisite for reliability.
Edsger Dijkstra, renowned Dutch computer scientist

....

Today's three Lessons, like all the Lessons, are an integral part of the Bohlen Program. Remember, no matter how simple Bob's Lessons are, they will combine to change your life. Today's Lessons were:

- **Just tell the truth**
- **Generally the simpler something is, the better it is**
- **A cluttered desk creates a cluttered mind**

Tomorrow's tasks:
Add today's Lessons to your card and remember to take it out several times a day to refresh your memory. If you think some of the Lessons are more important to you than others, put them at the top of your list and work harder on them.

If you were successful in your approach to your new mentor, tomorrow you will learn more about Daily Accountability and that will be something to share with your mentor. For now, you have taken the most important step you can.

If you have not been able to secure a mentor's help, you should place this at the top of your to-do list for tomorrow. The longer you leave it, the less time you will have to benefit from everything you are learning. ***This is the most important task you will perform!***

PHASE TWO

Personalizing the Program

DAY SEVEN
Daily Accountability works

Now that you have identified your mentor, it is time to learn more about how the process works. Remember what Bob already said, changing behavior is one of the most difficult things to do. It may improve your performance if someone you respect is interested in what you are doing, but that alone is not enough to guarantee that you will stay on course.

It would be easy to think that the mentor is responsible for making sure you fulfill your commitments, but Bob explains that this isn't how it works. "Most people would think that the Daily Accountability I negotiate with my students is for me, but it's really for my students to see whether or not they've accomplished what they wanted to each day. My program makes sure the person who has committed to a goal is really committed and that they stay on target. The role of a mentor is to be supportive, to talk with you about what you want to achieve and so on, but usually they don't have the authority to force you to do anything."

At this point you may be thinking, "Well, what reason would people have to do what they've committed to?." Bob's Lesson is:

Significant rewards and non rewards work every time if they are really meaningful

Bob explains further:
"The first time I ever focused on intently defining and quantifying goals was with Dr. Fred Grosse from New Zealand. We worked together a lot and I brought him to talk to my sales people and students many times over a ten-year period. He was the first coach I knew to figure out the system of defining rewards as 10s, 20s, 50s, and 100s."

Rewards

Bob explains his system of rewards as follows: "People often promise themselves a reward if they successfully complete a task. It's something we all do all the time, but in this system the reward is quantified to reflect how significant your achievement was. A 10 is easy. They're things that you really enjoy, but that don't cost much, if anything. They are things you could do two or three times a day to reward yourself for doing what you set out to do. Examples might be listening to your favorite music, having a glass of your best wine, going to a restaurant for dinner, or enjoying a special dessert. You might want to give something to somebody dear to you because sometimes it's more fun to give rewards than to get them. You know, a walk in the evening is something you can do together and it doesn't cost you anything! These are the kinds of things that you can do just by deciding to do them, something you would reward yourself for a great day."

"A 25 is a reward you would give yourself for a great month of being focused and achieving what you set out to accomplish during that time. For example, you might have negotiated a contract with a new customer and so you could take your family out to dinner at a really special restaurant. If you are a salesperson you might need to generate $10,000 in commissions in a month. If you make it, you might reward yourself with a weekend trip. Another 25 could be buying a new suit or outfit you have always wanted. As a rule I generally set a range for the 25s of ½% to 1% of my annual income."

"A 50 would be something you have always wanted to accomplish if you had a great year. You need to identify something that is really important to you. It could be a stock investment, an income property, a new car, a new home, or anything else that is important enough to you to be a 'once a year' reward or goal. The value of a 50 is often up to 5% of your annual income."

"Setting 100s is always the hardest for my coaching students to do. A 100 is a lifetime goal. It might be a level of passive income that will let someone slow down or retire, or an all-expenses-paid trip to Europe or the Orient for you and your entire family. It can be a second home in a resort area. These are just a few examples. The hardest part for me is getting people to write down their goals and then prioritize them so, as a coach, I can figure out what really is important to them and what isn't."

If you reflect on it, there are examples all around us of how this works. We all know that most students work under a system of rewards and non rewards. It's this simple: if students study enough to pass, they are rewarded with knowledge and a qualification that can help them for the rest of their life. If they don't study hard enough, they fail. Not only have they wasted their time and money, but they have to face the shame of being a failure and may end up working for the rest of their life in a career that never allows them to reach their full potential. These are powerful incentives and we know they work in the majority of cases because most students pass.

Another example everybody is familiar with is the process of buying a house. Getting a mortgage is probably the biggest financial commitment most people ever make, but the rewards are significant: owning your own home, the security and prestige of being a home-owner, and so on. The non rewards are also very powerful. If you fail to meet your financial obligations, you will lose your home and all the money you put into it. It will also severely reduce your chances of ever getting a mortgage again. Despite the recent housing loan meltdown, the truth is that these powerful incentives work and most people successfully follow through with their commitment to pay for their home.

Bob applies this same idea to rewards he negotiates with his students. "For example," he says, "I might say, 'If you remain daily accountable each day for six months, how are you going to reward yourself?' They come up with a reward that's really important. Some of them are really interesting. One of my students wanted to go and play golf at Troon in Scotland! Once the reward is set I keep them Daily Accountable, so they make more money because their priorities are in focus. Because of that they can afford the reward. The hardest part has been to get coaching students just to write down their dreams quantified as 10's, 25's, 50's, 100's. But it's been wonderful to see what happens when they do write them down and really focus on them. Literally one goal after another is achieved."

Rick Ferris once negotiated a reward that developed in stages, as he explains: "At a Bohlen conference in 2004 I wanted to develop strategies to increase my business, so I committed to 10 face-to-face client meetings a week for 25 weeks. The final reward was a $25,000 diamond ring for my wife on our 20th anniversary. That afternoon I bought the ring on lay away with $1,000 down, then I sent $1,000 a week as I completed the 10 faces. I achieved my goal on time and my wife got the ring!"

In fact Bob motivates himself in exactly the same way.

"I always have my goals written down. At the beginning of last year my wife Lillian and I wrote down 128 things we wanted to do and we scratched 117 off the list as we accomplished them. Every few months I evaluate what things I want to do and that motivates me to accomplish things. Going to Hong Kong, Shanghai and Tokyo last year was one. The amazing thing is that when people start writing down goals and targets, things that are really, really important to them, a light bulb goes on. They could do 10s every day, 25s every week, 50s every other month, and they could probably do 100s every year. A lot of them didn't think they could do any 100s in a lifetime! Significant rewards and non rewards work every time if they are really meaningful to the student."

Non rewards

Rewards will work for motivated people, but Bob knows that a lot of people just don't care enough to work at something until it's done.

"That's why rewards aren't enough," he says. "As I always say, changing people's behavior is one of the most difficult things to do. That's why you also have to have non-rewards in place. To keep my students on target I have to make sure I get the Daily Accountable sheets I mentioned on Day One. If I *don't* get those sheets each day, I assume they didn't do them. To make sure they submit them, I negotiate a 'non-reward' for not submitting. It has to be something so terrible that they would never let it happen. Usually I get them to write a check to me for an amount that they agree would be a strong disincentive. It may vary from $5,000 to $20,000 for each of those people. If they are Daily Accountable every day for the next three months, I send them the check back. If they aren't, I cash it."

It seems shocking, but Bob qualifies this statement: "In my entire coaching career I've only cashed three checks. This week at a coaching seminar with 25 mega real estate agents I collected checks for $200,000 as accumulated non-rewards for people not being daily accountable. That seems like a lot, but I'm confident I won't have to cash any of those checks – and of course I don't want to. Also, non-rewards don't have to be only about money. It can be not doing things that they like. We negotiate each one individually."

If this seems tough, Bob disagrees. "The *really* tough thing is to change people's behavior. It's one of the toughest things in life. Look at smoking and alcohol addicts, drug addicts, lazy people who don't really want to work, people who pass through life just existing and not excelling. If you've lived your life a certain way for many years, it's hard to change. The real task is to find a way to change people's behavior."

As an example of how non-rewards work, Bob recalls the man from Day Three who lost exactly 100 pounds weight. "I had him write a $50,000 check to me, which I could cash if he didn't achieve the weight loss on time. He lost the weight, so I tore up the check. It's easy for someone to just say they want to do something, but this really focuses their attention and guarantees a strong commitment from them."

"My students do this perfectly willingly," Bob points out. "I ask them how much they'd be willing to pay if they don't remain Daily Accountable. They are not forced to do anything. They know what will be meaningful to them and they agree to it. It's a measure of their commitment and it works every time. If they don't see the check cashed *and* they get the reward, they've *changed their behavior*."

You might be thinking that not everyone can write a check for $50,000 to their mentor. "They don't have to!" says Bob. "But there are other ways than writing checks to guarantee that somebody meets their commitments. All they have to do is agree to something that they would do anything to avoid. I work with a guy in Canberra, Australia, who earns millions, but his non-reward was putting on a swimsuit and washing all of the cars in the company parking lot. He performed every day for 30 days, so he didn't have to do it."

Another way might be for someone to write a letter to a prior employer who they really dislike. The letter could say that they hadn't appreciated him enough and they want to say he deserves recognition for what he does. Of course they don't believe it and they don't want him to get the letter, but the mentor keeps the letter and if they fail to remain Daily Accountable, the mentor sends it."

At first glance it seems harsh, but Bob explains why that isn't true. "It's something the student does willingly. The mentor has asked them to suggest the non-reward, not the other way around. The mentor doesn't want it to happen either, but there has to be a real threat of it happening, or it won't work. If somebody fails to perform and then doesn't follow through with the non reward, they are destroying the whole basis of the mentoring process. It is a waste of their time and the mentor's, and they'll either have to renegotiate a new non-reward, or the arrangement collapses. In my experience it doesn't happen."

Everything you have learned today is so important that, apart from Day One, this is the only day you will learn one Lesson:

> ▰ **Significant rewards and non rewards work every time if they are really meaningful**

Tomorrow's tasks:
You should talk to your mentor and explain the system of rewards and non rewards. Once they have fully understood the purpose of the Lesson, it's time to negotiate your own first agreed task. Look at the Lessons you have learned over the last seven days and choose a task that you think will have the most meaning for you.

If you want to be sure you can't cheat, choose a task that your mentor can easily verify. For example, on Day Two under the

Lesson *Start each day from zero*, you were told to write to-do lists for every day. When you are negotiating this with your mentor, show them the to-do lists you have already done, then agree that for the next week you will show them your daily to-do lists. Negotiate your reward and non reward, then stick to the plan and you get the reward. Don't do it and…well you know by now.

Another task your mentor can verify is *Always be early*. After all, they have to meet with you. Either you are early, on time, or late. It's that simple. You can even give them permission to contact your boss (assuming your mentor isn't your boss) to find out if you have been late for work.

If you are confident that you won't cheat yourself, you can choose a task that doesn't need to be verified. For example, you can suggest to your mentor that you'd like to start giving meaningful compliments every day. Agree on a target that is appropriate for you, such as, 'I will give out three compliments every day this week and that they will be sincere.' You need to keep note of each day's compliments so you can report on them every day or perhaps at the end of the week.

What will your negotiated reward be? That will depend on your personal circumstances. It should be something you can afford, so if you are still young and have just started on your path to success a night at the movies, or a night out doing something else you enjoy might work. If you have already achieved a degree of success, it might be something more substantial like a meal at a restaurant, or a new pair of shoes. You choose and discuss it with your mentor.

What will your non reward be? How about mowing your mentor's lawn? That's one that will work for anybody, and your mentor might like it too! You can also use Bob's system of writing checks. The point is that it has to be meaningful to you, or it won't work. You know your own circumstances best, so use your imagination.

Now you are starting to make yourself Daily Accountable. We'll learn more about this soon, but for now, take charge of this process, *have fun and don't let yourself down!*

DAY EIGHT
Building a positive attitude

From today you are Daily Accountable, so every Lesson you learn will mean much more because you are going to be able to put it into action on a daily basis and then have your performance verified.

Your first Lesson today is among the most powerful that Bob has to offer. It will have a profound effect on everything you do. We all know people who always see the downside of life. It only takes one chronic complainer and a whole group can be affected: a sports team, an office department, a group of friends. Somebody starts complaining about something and others will soon agree. Before long the whole conversation turns negative. Bob's Lesson is once more very simple:

Eliminate negativity

It doesn't take long with Bob to discover that he likes to surround himself with what he calls *positive energy*. "I learned a long time ago," he says, "that whatever energy you put out in the world will come back to you time and time again. If you are positive and you help people, when you need it they will be there to help you. People who are upbeat attract the same type of people. Just try getting on an airplane with a happy smile and see how others respond to you. If you smile, they smile."

Bob is equally sure that it is necessary to remove all the negative influences from your life. "I see people get in what I call 'victim mode' all the time and they bring in other victims around them. I say, if something goes wrong, *don't have a pity party for yourself*. It happens to everybody all the time. Over the years I've seen so many people burn out in their careers due to the toxic people they live with or pal around with. One of the most important things you can do in your life is eliminate negativity. If people around you are negative it affects your psychological outlook, your performance, *and* it affects your happiness! In contrast, if you are busy, active and have a full life, you overcome adversity. My belief is that life isn't a dress rehearsal. You only do it once, so you need to do it right and you *should have fun while you are doing it.*"

That's my gift. I let that negativity roll off me like water off a duck's back. If it's not positive, I didn't hear it. If you can overcome that, fights are easy.
George Foreman, the oldest man to win a
heavyweight boxing title, at 45 years of age

"It's the same with marriage," Bob adds. "When people work at their jobs incessantly, often it's because they don't want to go home. One of my great friends was in a toxic marriage for fifteen years. He worked like a burro and he was always talking about sex, which is a sure sign he wasn't having much. I hammered him for ten years about his obvious unhappiness. Finally he saw the light, moved out, and filed for divorce. In the space of a few months I saw an amazing transformation. He was always smiling, took time for friends, was always holding hands with his new girlfriend and in the most difficult of times his business grew because even more people wanted to enjoy his positive energy and do business with him."

Bob works with Tom Droste to help improve Tom's effectiveness in his software company. Tom agrees completely with Bob about removing negativity from his life. "Negativity is all around us," Tom says, "and it saps your strength every day. We can all complain as much as we want, but by focusing on the positive we can accomplish great things. I've known Bob for five years and don't think I've heard him complain about more than five things in that time, and each time it was short and then on to something positive. When I'm with Bob and I want to complain, I try to think of something positive to talk about and every time my energy is increased. He has that effect on people. Anybody can do it. You just have to think of something positive, or change the conversation to a positive one, and everyone around you will be energized."

Bob repeats this message to his associates over and over. He is confident it will make an unbelievable difference to their happiness, energy and performance. With typical bluntness he states his case: "When I don't like somebody, I just don't work with them." Importantly, when people show him they are positive and want to get something done, then he is happy to help them do that. "We feed on each other's energy," says Bob, "and that's what makes the process successful."

As you go through your day tomorrow, look carefully at each person you spend time with. Ask yourself, "Is the way they live their life helpful to themselves or to me?" Everybody can have a bad day, but we are talking about people who only have bad days. Think about how they see life and if you believe they are consistently being negative, you should start making plans. *Get them out of your life and move on!*

Bob has another Lesson that is the flipside of what we just learned.

Invest your energy where it will be appreciated and rewarded

It is Bob's belief that once you start spending your time with positive people, it rubs off. You'll start to see life in a whole new light and, once again, the positive feedback loop kicks in.

Others will become aware of your positive attitude and will respond to you in new ways.

Mark Herman is once again in complete agreement with what Bob says: "You only have so many waking hours or so much energy, so using them where they are not appreciated or rewarded is a waste of both. You need to find a better place to use your energy, and I am talking both psychologically and monetarily."

Mark recalls how when he was young he had an experience that changed his life. "I was working with a bank and unknown to me the boss had been watching me. One day he really surprised me when he said, 'You've been doing a very good job.' Soon I was put into the queue to become president of one of our banks. I was only 29 at the time and an opportunity for someone of that age was almost unheard of. Then one day I was unexpectedly called by a very senior executive in our company who offered me the job. He said, 'It's a big step, do you think you can handle it?' I said I could, went through the interview process and was selected. It was life-changing and I've never forgotten it. The key thing was that it was totally unsolicited and came as a great surprise to me, but it happened because I had put my energy where it was appreciated."

Today's Lessons were:

- **Eliminate negativity**
- **Invest your energy where it will be appreciated and rewarded**

Tomorrow's tasks:
It's time to step back and observe the people around you. Ask yourself how you feel after you have been with them? Energized and stimulated? Score *plus one*. Tired and deflated? Score *minus one*. You need to start making decisions

about who you spend time with and how you will deal with people who may be dragging you down.

The next list might be better kept to yourself, but you need to write down the people who you are probably better off not spending time with. If you can't think of anybody, that's great, so you can move on to the next list of who most appreciates what you do. *These are the people you need to spend time with.*

Your to-do list should also include writing down the ways you can more usefully allocate your time and energy. Keep notes of what you do with your day and at the end of the day review what you have done. It should be clear. Either you are using your time well, or you are wasting time. This is going to be very important as we will soon be developing your Ideal Day and Ideal Week plans. Get the habit now: *eliminate negativity and target your energy!*

If you are meeting with your mentor, it's time to report in. Remember, it's all about *Daily Accountability.* You know what you agreed to do, so now you should be able to report that you successfully fulfilled the commitment. If you negotiated a reward for completing the first day, enjoy! If you agreed that you would complete a task every day for a week, scratch one day off!

If you did not complete your agreed task, you need to take a serious look at your commitment. After all, it is only your first day of Daily Accountability. You should talk to your mentor about how you can avoid this happening again. Then it's time to put your non reward into action. *It's not worth it, is it?*

Before you finish the day, you should think about what you are next going to negotiate with your mentor. You don't have to renegotiate a fresh set of tasks every day, but you do need to report every day on progress.

DAY NINE
Taking responsibility

Yesterday you learned about eliminating negativity from your life. If you follow that Lesson alone, it will change your life. However, there's never any guarantee that you'll always have a perfect day. Everybody fails sometimes and if you do make a mistake, it won't help if you try to hide it. But you can make things better by facing up to what has happened. Bob's Lesson to help you here is:

If you encounter a problem, look in the mirror

Bob's explanation for this Lesson is very personal. "It took me years to learn that when I got really upset or mad with someone on my team, the problem was mostly mine. In reality the problem was *me*! It might have been because I didn't give them the proper direction or the right kind of leadership. Maybe I didn't focus on a certain detail I should have, or I didn't do something I should have done a few weeks before. Perhaps I didn't check to see that someone else had completed their job assignment."

"I've always understood the buck stops with me. People sometimes only hear the good news and don't ask enough questions to get the bad news. If something doesn't close, or if a client is upset with our service, I'm ultimately responsible. Just try it. When a deal fails, or you get mad, or when there is a major dilemma, objectively look in the mirror. I always say e*go gets in the way of progress and success more often than you can imagine.*"

Once more, Rick Ferris confirms Bob's advice: "I've learned that if I am not getting enough business, there's no point blaming the people I'm dealing with. The only place to look for a solution is in the mirror. It could be my attitude, or maybe I'm just going through the motions and not really expecting a good result. One thing is for sure, if I keep getting the same bad result over and over again, then it's not somebody else! It can only be me and I have to make a change. It's too easy to blame external things or other people, but the fact is that you have to look at what *you* are doing and make the changes you need to."

If Michael Edlen identifies where a problem is, if it was something caused by his staff, he doesn't like to criticize those who were involved. "If one of my staff drops the ball, I point out to them that fixing it is not personal, it's the system. I believe that if we didn't function well as a team, then we have to find a way to tweak the system. By changing procedures, we can always do better."

If you do determine that something is your own fault, Bob has another Lesson that will help you deal with it in the simplest way possible:

An apology is the superglue to life

"An apology is the superglue to life," Bob says, "because it can repair anything. Sometimes it is so easy to make a good impression. Hardly any feud, dispute, upset, or trauma can't be resolved by one party apologizing to the other. They just need to say, *I was wrong*, or *I was stupid, I shouldn't have thought that*."

Apologizing comes hard to many people, but Bob thinks it is too important to overlook. "I think I learned it very early in life," Bob replied. "When I was playing basketball I learned that if you make a mistake, or you take a bad shot, you need to take responsibility. If you say, 'Guys, that was my fault, I'm sorry,' you build better teamwork than if you act like it wasn't your fault."

This Lesson is just as important in business as it is in sporting life. Bob knows that some people avoid apologizing because they think it is an admission of guilt. "In fact," he says, "sometimes it can get you out of serious trouble. I've seen it time and time again. When people are wronged, if the person who wronged them simply apologizes, no legal action follows. There are so many cases where people sued somebody just because they wanted to make sure they apologized."

....

An apology is a good way to have the last word.
author unknown

....

It's human nature to be defensive when you are criticized, so the best way to avoid it is to look closely at yourself and adjust your behavior before others feel the need to comment.

These two important Lessons are about taking responsibility for yourself:

- **If you encounter a problem, look in the mirror**
- **An apology is the superglue to life**

Tomorrow's tasks:

Now you are starting to accumulate Lessons, the need to prioritize is becoming more important. As Bob says, you have to prioritize your tasks to maximize efficiency. Some of the Lessons should already be starting to be automatic. For example, once you start seeing the positive results, it very quickly becomes second nature to give compliments every day. Also, by now you should understand the importance of being on time and you should be accountable to your mentor on that point. These are examples of things that you probably don't need to write on your daily to-do list now, although you will need to revise and check progress later on. We will deal with that later, but now we need to set tomorrow's task.

Take some time during the day to examine how you react when you encounter a problem. Do you try to shift blame to others? Consider what the consequences would be if you accepted responsibility for a problem. They are almost certainly less harmful than you think. You might be surprised to find that others are even more willing to step up and share the responsibility with you. Even more surprising, you might find yourself gaining more respect than if you keep quiet or try to shift blame.

Discuss this with your mentor and if you think it is appropriate, plan on taking responsibility or apologizing when it is clear that you made a mistake. It's much easier than you think and it also eliminates potential negativity from your day. This is another Lesson you can negotiate with your mentor, so you can add it to your Daily Accountability list.

DAY TEN
It's all in the mind

Over the last nine days you have learned some simple but effective ways to change how you interact with those around you. The tasks you were given for today include examining whether you are taking responsibility for your own actions. Of course, how you act depends to a large extent on how you think about yourself, so your state of mind affects everything you do.

Bob has already shown how hard it is to change a person's behavior. Habits usually develop over many years and people become dependent on them, unquestioningly following the same patterns. Changing behavior requires changing how people think. Bob's Lesson is:

Life and business are all mental

"What people feel is often in their head and is not reality," he explains. "I believe that if we think we can do something, we can. Also, if we think we don't have a chance of doing it, we don't. The hardest and most difficult distance we travel is the 5" between our ears. So that's the starting point. You hear from mountain climbers who go up Mt. Everest that what gets them to the top is their mental outlook, not necessarily the physical things. The best example is the 4-minute mile barrier. One person broke it then how many did it after that? It was just a mental barrier and once that fell it meant nothing."

* * *

Whether you think you can
or think you can't – you are right.
Henry Ford

* * *

"Nobody believes it," says Bob, "but I'm really lazy. I find it easy to put things off till tomorrow, so that's why I have to remain focused on what I need to do to get things done. I can't tell you how important it is to develop the ability to stay focused on what you want, whether it's in business or in your private life, and that it is all mental."

••

The pool is terrible, but that doesn't have much to do with my record swims. That's all mental attitude.
Mark Spitz,who won seven gold medals
at the 1972 Olympics

••

On day four we learned how important it is to avoid negative people. It's also important to work on maintaining a positive state of mind for ourselves. Here's another Lesson to help you do that:

Avoid the emotional roller coaster

Bob calls this dealing with "the mental ups and downs of life." He explains: "It really takes lots of mental strength to deal with our daily challenges. A skill I have developed, and that I now find essential, is being able to park my most significant challenge outside of my daily activities. I really believe we get back the same type of energy we send out. You can't get people to enjoy being with you or to do business with you by telling them all of your problems, or even acting like you have any problems. If we are worried, or in victim mode about something, we collect other people who are in the same mode. People prefer to be with people who are upbeat, positive, direct and honest, particularly in business. The art of being upbeat and positive requires parking negative things outside of your head during business hours."

Bob gives this personal example of how he eliminates negativity from his life: "For me, one of the most frustrating things I have to deal with is my annual IRS audit. It occurs again and again, even though the total adjustments of my tax return to date have been almost non-existent. Clearly, when someone earns lots of money they become a target, but in fact only once in my whole business career have I met with an IRS agent to discuss my personal return. Usually I deal with it by having my CPA and tax attorney, or my personal assistant meet with them. I just park it outside of my head."

A recent example of something that happened to one of Bob's coaching students reinforces this idea. "He had an ethics complaint filed against him," Bob explains. "In my opinion it was not justified, but he had never had anything like that happen before. It started to consume him and get him off track. I said, 'Stop! Take an hour, no more, and prepare your response for the hearing. Then put it out of your mind until the morning of the hearing.' He did that and got back on track with his personal production. Three weeks later the hearing was held, he was quickly vindicated, and it was over. If he had stayed obsessed with the process he would have been off-track for three weeks and it would have cost him tens of thousands of dollars in commissions."

Bob has a simple strategy that he often uses to deal with problems like this. "I write down the biggest challenge I have at the moment, then tear it up and throw it in the waste basket. Maybe it is just symbolic, but I find it helps clear my mind of that challenge."

It's important to remember that no matter how hard you try, life is not all smooth sailing. Despite our best efforts we inevitably make mistakes, but in fact we need to fail, as Bob explains with this Lesson:

It's our failures we learn from, not our successes

Looking back on bad experiences is not always comfortable, but Bob insists that you can benefit from even the worst events: "Anyone who is successful, really successful, has had lots of failures and makes lots of mistakes. It seems to me that I never learn much from my successes, only these failures. I'll never forget what I learned in my first real job. My boss said to me one day 'Bob, I learned a long time ago that everyone makes mistakes, but you are a pretty dumb S.O.B if you get stung by the same bee in the same place twice!'."

··

There are no secrets to success. It is the result of preparation, hard work, and learning from failure.
Colin Powell

··

Even after all his years of success, Bob admits he can still make mistakes. "My most recent learning experience was when a small group of us bought a building company that had a good history and a good balance sheet. I had always had a lot of respect for the owner, but it turned out he had doctored the books and capitalized lots of expenses that should have been written off. When the 2008 meltdown hit, sales drastically declined and my share of the lesson cost me millions. Good thing I didn't quit my day job! The two lessons I learned were: no more recourse debt, and stick to what you do best. I know I'm good at sales, but maybe I am not so good at building houses. Although we have just sold 16 new homes this month in a bad market, at that rate it will take us over 4 years to recover the loss. Lesson learned."

I have missed more than 9000 shots in my career.
I have lost almost 300 games. On 26 occasions
I have been entrusted to take the game winning shot...
and missed. I have failed over and over and over
again in my life, and that is why I succeed.
Michael Jordan, acclaimed as the
greatest basketball player of all time

Today is the tenth day of the Bohlen plan and you are one third of the way to completion! Today we talked about how to strengthen your state of mind to overcome the ups and downs of life. Tomorrow we will learn some more strategies to further develop your mental focus. For now, before you write down tomorrow's tasks, let's remind ourselves of what you learned today:

- **Life and business are all mental**
- **Avoid the emotional roller coaster**
- **It's our failures we learn from, not our successes**

Tomorrow's tasks:

Now that you have reached the ten-day mark, it's a good time to review what you have learned, revisit the Lessons that are most important for you, and to confirm your tasks and strategies with your mentor.

1. Write down a new list of all the Lessons you have learned so far, then go through the list and underline those Lessons you think you have learned the most from.

2. If there are any Lessons that you have not yet acted on, or failed to follow up on as much as you think you should have, mark them with a large **X**. Make a separate list of those Lessons. Remember, don't avoid any just because

you think they would be too much trouble. They are probably the Lessons you need the most!

3. Discuss these Lessons with your mentor. You need to identify the most important ones and negotiate your rewards and non rewards.

Don't forget, you need to discuss every day's performance with your mentor to remain Daily Accountable.

DAY ELEVEN
Looking ahead

Yesterday Bob told us about learning from our failures. However, while he believes that we should learn from the past, we should never be obsessed with it. That's why he always starts each day at zero – it allows him to focus on what he can change. The Lesson is:

Live in the future, not in the past.

Yesterday we saw how Bob made an uncharacteristically bad choice when he purchased a building company, but he is convinced that he will benefit from the experience in the long term. "If you aren't looking to the future, he says, "you really don't have much to live for." So although Bob believes that decisions need to be based upon what you have learned in the past, this is not the same as *dwelling* in the past. It's about learning, says Bob: "Too many people let the same things happen to them over and over again, but until you learn the lesson that you are being handed, internalize it and put it to use, you don't move forward to the next level."

....

*Look to the future, because that is where
you'll spend the rest of your life.*
George Burns, entertainer.

....

Michael Edlen tells us that he really appreciates Bob's knack of looking ahead of where things are at the moment. He explains: "Preparation is critical for success. Sometimes when the market takes off we're not ready to take advantage of it. It's the same when the market slows down. The key is getting there before the others. Wayne Gretsky once said that the reason he was a great hockey player was because he was always heading to where the puck was going to be, rather than going to where it was. He was ahead of the game."

The message is clear. *Look ahead.* The good news is that once you start looking ahead you will automatically raise your sights and you will see where you are going. Bob believes we should always:

Start with the end in mind and work backwards

Many of Bob's Lessons have the same simple truths at their core and the need to plan is a recurring theme. He believes that if you don't plan, you don't know where you are going. "So many times,' he told me, "I've gotten involved with people on projects only to discover that there was no final objective in mind. People get all hung up on the process of going somewhere rather than focusing on where they are going and their end point."

• •

Most of us serve our ideals by fits and starts.
The person who makes a success of living is one who
sees his goal steadily and aims for it unswervingly.
Cecil B. DeMille, one of the most successful
movie directors of all time

• •

Bob has this recent example: "Recently we met with a very talented artist and acquired a piece from him. When I asked him where he wanted to be in five years he had no idea. After discussing the subject for a while he said he thought he'd like a larger studio with ten-foot ceilings so he could paint larger works. We then talked about how hard it is to sell really large works because most people have limited wall space.

Pretty soon he saw that the only customers for larger pieces were going to be museums or corporate collectors with tall ceilings and lots of wall space. We talked some more and he concluded that his real objective was to be an independent artist, and that meant he had to be financially independent. To do that he needed to create smaller, more universally appealing pieces. Finally we all agreed that his short-term end point was to get out of his parents' basement into his own space, and that would help him create work that would sell more easily, not larger pieces which there is little or no market for."

Doug Ferguson works in the Atlanta Georgia area and has a remarkable track record of success in the real estate industry. He has known Bob for ten years and he agrees with everything Bob says on this point. Doug uses the analogy of a road trip: "If I want to get to Texas," he says, "I'll start by finding Texas on the map. All the roads in between are the stages that will get me there, but I have to know where I'm going. It's true for your life dreams, but it's also true at a simpler level, such as the conversations you have with your clients. If I don't ask sellers how much they want to net at the end of a transaction, I don't know how to start planning the process. When I'm talking to a buyer, I need to know things such as where they want to live. For example, a client may want to live in a specific school district. You always work backwards from these end goals."

Bob has another Lesson on this:

The number one reason most people don't get what they want is that they don't know what they want

"When I ask people where they want to be 5 years from now," says Bob, "many times they can't imagine being any place very different than they are now. But if I ask them to close their eyes and believe they've just won the $100,000,000 lottery, then to open their eyes and write down what they'd do with the money, they can do that really easily. The amazing thing is that very often they write down things that don't cost very much and that they *could be doing now!* But they don't think they can because they believe it's beyond their means. Their ability to dream has shut down and they accept what's already there. As I always say, *life is all mental.* I could give hundreds of examples of coaching students who have written down many things and then achieved them all. They used to think 'I just couldn't afford that,' or 'We could never do that,' when in reality it was within their reach."

As we have seen before, Bob returns again and again to the need to *change your behavior.* If you are not happy with how you are living your life, something has to change. The only thing in life you have control over is your own behavior, so that is why this underpins all of Bob's Lessons.

Today's Lessons were:

- **Live in the future, not in the past.**
- **Start with the end in mind and work backwards**
- **The number one reason most people don't get what they want is that they don't know what they want**

Tomorrow's tasks:

Earlier we discussed writing down important Lessons on a card and carrying it with you. By now you know enough Lessons that you might consider making separate cards to carry on different days. If you list around five Lessons on each card, it enables you to focus more on those you think are most important and it makes them that much more achievable. Refer to the list often, think about how you can apply each Lesson, then *act on it!*

Today's Lessons strongly reinforce what you learned on Day Two when you listed your dreams. It's time to revisit your earlier list of dreams and refocus on it. Now that you are becoming more familiar with the Bohlen Program, you can refine your list and discuss it again with your mentor. Remember, *raise your sights and you will amaze yourself!*

DAY TWELVE
Taking even more control of your life

Yesterday we talked about the importance of looking to the future. People who are negative about life often find reasons not to try a new approach. How often have you heard someone say, 'We tried that before and it didn't work.' Sometimes they sound almost satisfied about the fact that something failed. Often if you suggest a new idea to other people, they'll say, 'Well, I don't know. We've never done that before....' Bob firmly believes that if you want to achieve anything, you need to take responsibility for what you do. Sometimes this means making choices that seem tough, but you will learn that these choices are going to make your life easier, not tougher. Bob doesn't waste words when he offers this Lesson:

Successful people believe 'I create my life.'
Unsuccessful people believe 'Life happens to me.'

Bob explains the difference between these two groups of people as follows: "Most people who accumulate a lot of wealth do so by coming up with an idea, a system, or a product. Maybe they did it by managing a business or an investment, but most of them had a plan. Unfortunately, there are a lot of people who don't think they need a plan. Many young people today have a huge sense of entitlement. Part of that is because their parents have given them way too much and have spoiled them rotten."

Bob's example of this is about somebody he knows who owns a large company. "He just drove his son to Florida for school and left him with $5,000 in his bank account. He then told me his son really didn't appreciate it very much. I said to him

'Well, why the hell should he appreciate it? The bottom line is you gave it all to him!' People often don't appreciate what you give to them. They take it for granted, but they'll never really appreciate it unless they earn it."

Most people would say that they can't be in control of their life *all* the time. Bob agrees, "But that's no reason to be afraid to take control of what you can. You do what you can." Bob's Lesson here is typically realistic:

Change what you can change and accept the rest

He explains: "Certain things are controlled by factors that you can have no impact on. I can't change the fact that the sun rises in the east and sets in the west, so I accept that as a condition and I operate on a schedule that takes that into consideration. Similarly, I have no impact on the rate of foreclosures on home loans in the United States. But I can take advantage of the fact that there are a lot of homes being foreclosed on by brokering them, finding new home owners to buy them and helping the old home owners get them sold."

Wade Micoley runs his own successful real estate business in Wisconsin and he has been coached by Bob for several years. Wade agrees that it is a waste of time to dwell on things you can't do anything about: "Time is our most valuable resource and we need to use our mental and physical energy on things that are within our control. As Bob always says, a lot of what happens is beyond our control, such as interest rates, the economy, bankers, taxes, even the weather! Most people complain about things they have no control over, but that only takes your energy away from changing what you can."

In contrast with this idea, most of us know someone who worries so much about doing the best they can, that they set unrealistic expectations for themselves. It's effectively the same as worrying about what you can't change and Bob believes it almost guarantees failure:

Perfection equals procrastination

"In my experience," says Bob, "anybody who wants things perfect, never gets there. They keep trying to get them perfect, but they never get to the end of the line. I've got perfectionists working for me and in many areas they do very well, but they don't get as much done in a day as I do. I delegate a pile of things to other people and even though not all of them come back perfect, if I had tried to get all that detail right I wouldn't have got anything done. Decision makers and senior executives who run major companies know they are not going to be perfect with every decision. The objective is to make a lot more right decisions than wrong decisions so that your batting average is strong. I'll give you a great example of this. We got fifty listings from a bank last week and my assistant Regina's job was to assign them. My son Scott got involved and he is a perfectionist to a degree. He wanted to figure out which agent ought to get each listing. After an hour and half he'd assigned two listings. Regina said, 'Why don't you just go on and let me do the rest.' In five minutes she'd assigned the other forty-eight. She knew that 'this falls into that slot and that falls into this slot.' It might be a little sloppy, but at least she got them all in slots quickly and efficiently."

•••

I have always found that if I move with seventy-five percent or more of the facts that I usually never regret it. It's the guys who wait to have everything perfect that drive you crazy.
Lee Iacocca, American businessman known for his
revival of the Chrysler Corporation in the 1980s

•••

Today's Lessons were:

- ▰ **Successful people believe "I create my life." Unsuccessful people believe "Life happens to me."**
- ▰ **Change what you can change and accept the rest**
- ▰ **Perfection equals procrastination**

Review: Today you should have completed the new list of your goals and discussed it with your mentor. If you fail to complete any of these tasks, you risk the chance of falling behind. Remember, Accountability is the only thing that will guarantee you stay on course.

Tomorrow's tasks:

Let's build on the Lesson, *Change what you can and accept the rest*. Remember what Bob said on Day Ten: "What people feel is often in their head and is not reality." It's time for a reality check.

Make a list of all the things that you'd like to be different in your life. As with all of these lists, don't hold back. It is as much about raising your awareness as anything else, so put all of your fantasies down as well. Your list might include your job, where you live, your life partner, your car, what you are studying, your appearance, your finances – you get the picture.

Take your time and when you have completed your list, put it to one side, take a clean sheet of paper and divide it down the middle. Write 'realistic' on one side and 'unrealistic' on the other. Then you need to copy things from your original list to the new divided list.

This may seem like an overly simple exercise, but remember what Bob said about writing things down. It can make them more real and will focus your attention on what you need to do. If you are 5' 4" tall and you wrote, 'I'd like to be

6' tall,' you have to admit it's not realistic. On the other hand, if you wrote 'I'd like to lose 50 pounds, that's something you can achieve if you work systematically towards it. That's a *goal*. The same applies if you wrote, 'I'd like a Porsche,' or anything else that is attainable through the success you can achieve by following the Bohlen Program.

The unrealistic side of the page contains the things you need to get out of your head as they only take up time and mental energy. Remember what Bob said about things he doesn't want to interfere with his life. "I just park them outside of my head."

DAY THIRTEEN
Expanding your horizons

Today we are going to look at big-picture ideas to improve the quality of your life. Although it would be hard to find anyone more focused on business, it would be a mistake to think that Bob only spends his life working. Every day he finds time to do many different things that enrich his life. It is fascinating to hear how his passion for life grew from an early age.

"I always had a good example set for me," says Bob, "and my parents always told me, and my brothers and sisters, we could be anything we wanted to be. My father was a vocational agricultural teacher and coach in Bethany, Illinois. When I was five years old my dad decided we needed to move out of the 'big city,' even though it only had a population of 700, so we moved into my dad's folks' farmhouse in Moweaqua, Illinois. That's where my agricultural life began."

"On my fifth birthday my dad loaded me into the cab of our farm truck and we drove ten miles to my uncle's farm. Dad told me to go into the house and said he'd be in shortly. Soon he came in and said he was ready to leave. Outside he took me behind the truck and lifted me up. I could see two Shorthorn heifers, one red and the other white. He said I could have my pick of the two heifers, so I took the red one. Then my dad said I'd have to sign a note for her purchase, and I'd have to repay it with her first heifer calf or her first two bull calves. I'd also have to help by feeding them, cleaning the stalls, and so on. I named my calf Clipper."

··

> *Few things can help an individual more than to place*
> *responsibility on him, and to let him know that you trust him.*
> Booker T. Washington, author and early leader
> of the African-American community

··

That might seem like a lot of responsibility for a five-year-old, but Bob is convinced it was just this kind of experience that accounts for much of his early success. "A year and a half later Clipper had her first calf, a heifer, and my first loan was repaid. Eleven years later, when I was a freshman in college, we sold our herd at our farm dispersal sale and my share was $36,400. With that, plus working full-time at the University of Illinois cattle barns and a couple of scholarships, I got a degree and had $16,000 in cash left over to start out."

Bob's experience with his father sounds a lot like Daily Accountability and he believes that is true. "My dad made sure that I understood my responsibilities. I had to care for Clipper every day and I had to plan my day around that because I was accountable to him. It's a lesson that I've never forgotten, plus the fact that there is no better investment than in more education. I built my career on the education that Clipper helped pay for and I've never stopped educating myself ever since. I've always believed that when we stop learning and stop contributing, for whatever reason, life often ends, but as long as we have something to contribute to the world, and we are learning, we get to hang around."

Invest in your own education

"Take my own education," says Bob. "It never stops. I'm seventy, but I still go to at least twelve different seminars or conferences a year. I go to an event or two a week about real estate, art, or something else that interests me. This week I spent a day at the University of Michigan Museum of Art and I'll be at a real estate seminar this weekend. It's always proven to be the best investment I make."

....

*Intellectual growth should commence
at birth and cease only at death.*
Albert Einstein.

....

"I read at least two books a week, I watch the news on TV every morning, and I'm always going to exhibitions and art shows, not to be sociable, but to see what artists are doing and which artists intrigue me. I'm always challenged to learn more. That's the reason I coach business and real estate sales people around the world – the coach always learns the most."

Bob believes these educational activities should be quantified in your business plan: "That means where you are going to spend your time, energy and money getting educated. You need to work at developing your ability to control your life and that's done by learning as much as you can. One reason why it needs to be quantified is that many people don't really learn as much as they think they are. I often see 500 people at a seminar getting all hyped up and leaving filled with good intentions, but I know that maybe ten of them will act on what they have learned. It's really, really hard to change people's behavior. That's why you need a system to make sure you incorporate new ideas into your action plan and my way of guaranteeing that is Daily Accountability."

....

> *Formal education will make you a living;*
> *self education will make you a fortune.*
> Jim Rohn, business philosopher

....

Bob is very proud of how much he has donated to art museums, especially the University of Michigan Museum of Art. He also chaired the committee that raised nearly $100,000,000 for their impressive new building and was deeply involved with its design. Bob's contributions are not limited to art museums and even include giving money to the Detroit Zoo to bring a specialist from Africa to work at the zoo. "I've probably given money away to a hundred causes," he says proudly, "mostly to things that I think will improve the quality of people's lives when I'm gone."

With all this in mind, one of Bob's most valued personal Life Lessons is:

Surround yourself with art, it provides an environment and energy that fosters creativity

To explain this Lesson, Bob recalls his college years. "I must have walked by the Krannert Art Museum at the University of Illinois thousands of times during the four years I was in college, but I never went inside! I had no interest because I couldn't imagine there was anything in there I'd want to see. So when we designed the new University of Michigan Museum of Art addition, it was our idea to structure it so the students had to walk under and through it, so they'd look inside. It's glass, all open so students will see it when they cross the quadrangle to go to the student union. The hope is that they'll see enough things to get them to come in to learn and appreciate some real art."

*Every time a student walks past a really urgent,
expressive piece of architecture that belongs to
his college, it can help reassure him that he does
have that mind, does have that soul.*

Louis Kahn, architect

Bob firmly believes that his interest in art has changed how he lives. "I think art has a very positive influence on people's creativity and their lives once they begin to understand it and focus on it. It happened to me. In 1962 I saw a Tiffany lamp that I liked, so I bought it. This was when nobody else wanted Tiffany lamps. The first thing I'd always do when I came home was turn on the lamp because I loved the peaceful energy and primary colors it sent out. I bought several more after that and I progressed from there. Now I've visited over one hundred museums around the world and I'm still learning."

Art washes from the soul the dust of everyday life.

Pablo Picasso

Of course it's impossible for a businessman like Bob not to consider the financial implications of buying and selling art, as he confirms: "Over recent years I've bought millions worth of African art. I've since sold a portion of the collection for way more than I paid for the whole collection, but I still have 110 really great pieces left."

Bob's passion for art also extends from his private life into his working environment, as he explains: "If you surround people with art in the place where they work, it encourages a more creative psyche. The best way to determine that, and I've done it often, is to remove a piece from a specific area and see how people react. Most times they will say, 'Gosh, I really miss that piece!' What they are really saying is that they miss the energy they are given from the piece."

....

The arts are an even better barometer
of what is happening in our world than the
stock market or the debates in congress.
Hendrik Willem Van Loon,
Dutch American author

....

Doug Ferguson has been inspired by Bob's passion for collecting and has become a discerning collector of wood art himself. "Part of my dream, and it's a dream that I learned from Bob, is to surround myself with great art. We had this dream of putting art together and living with our own collection. Now we live in what is our own personal gallery and when I see this art every day it motivates me to go out and work those extra hours. You have to have a reason to work and this is one part of my dream that inspires me. You can't just work for money because it's not tangible. It's got to be for something greater. It can be helping people, or travel for example. In my case, part of my dream is about art. We've met a lot of great artists and have memories of those occasions that are so precious. I'll look at a piece of art and remember where I was and who I was with when I bought that piece."

In some ways these two Lessons are different from the other Lessons Bob offers, but that doesn't mean they are less important. They are both the kind of never-ending Lessons that will benefit you in unexpected ways for the rest of your life:

- ■ **Invest in your own education**
- ■ **Surround yourself with art, it provides an environment and energy that fosters creativity**

Tomorrow's tasks:

Tomorrow you get to spend some time on things that are very different from the other tasks you will be assigned. If you feel you didn't get what you wanted out of your education, it's never too late to try again. You can start on a modest scale and if you discover something that inspires you enough, it will grow. Try looking for educational opportunities for yourself during the coming days. It may be a seminar you can book yourself into, or a book you have always wanted to find the time to read. You can visit a bookshop during your lunch break and see what interests you there, or check out the continuing education opportunities at your local community college. Go on! **Challenge yourself!**

As you walk down the street tomorrow, step into that gallery you always walk past and see what you can find. If you are not used to thinking about art, then you have a new educational opportunity. Ask the gallery owner to talk to you about the art they are showing. It's about opening your mind to new ideas and new energy. It may be that music inspires you more. It might be dance, or literature. The most important thing is to remember that these two lessons go together. Don't just listen to the same music, watch the same movies, settle with a favorite painting. Make the effort to learn more, stretch your mind and your imagination. It's about looking at the big picture.

DAY FOURTEEN
Feeling and looking like success

By now you will be seeing the results of putting the Bohlen Program into action. It may simply be that people you meet each day feel happier to see you because you are noticing them more, or it may be because you are feeling a greater sense of achievement at the end of each day as you cross off all the things you have achieved. Once the positive feedback loop starts working, you will feel more and more energized and your sense of well-being will grow accordingly.

On Day Four you were asked you to keep the pages that record what you have achieved each day. Now that you are two weeks into the Bohlen Program, you should have accumulated an impressive list of prioritized tasks that you have achieved. They are the tangible record of how you are changing your life.

It's time to congratulate yourself!

Before we move on, file away these early lists as they are a valuable reference for assessing future progress. Continue making these daily lists of prioritized tasks and keep them all for now.

Yesterday we talked about stretching your mind by investing in your own education. It may have surprised you to learn that sometimes education is free and can be as simple as going into a gallery and asking questions. There are educational opportunities all around you.

The body is just like the mind and the old adage 'use it or lose it' applies equally to both. Now it's time to think about your body and improving how you feel:

If you are not stretching both your mind and body, they are shrinking

At most of the seminars run by Bob for real estate high-achievers it is surprising how much time is spent talking about health initiatives. Bob has extensively researched this area and has developed a distinct dislike of how drug companies have taken over the health agenda. He believes strongly in the ability of the body to heal and care for itself, and much of what he does is based on this simple philosophy.

"Before my father, nobody in my family lived past about 55, so I never thought much about being around when I was 70, or even 100. Then about fifteen years ago I started to think seriously about these things. For example, a great book on the subject is *Breakthrough* by Suzanne Somers. Now I take a lot of care. If I'm healthy I can accomplish more and contribute more. That also means exercising. I don't like it, but it's something you have to do. I work out regularly with a personal trainer. Your muscles are like your mind, if you don't exercise they shrink and atrophy."

Bob also changed the way he thinks about nutrition and sleep. "How much you sleep," he says" is related to what you eat during the course of the day. Most of your body's energy is used to digest what you eat. You shouldn't eat a lot and you should eat only protein *or* only carbohydrates at a single meal. Your body secretes different enzymes to digest them, so if you just eat one of them your body only has to work half as hard because it just secretes the enzyme to digest what you ate – proteins or carbohydrates. Also, if you don't drink liquids with meals, you don't wash the enzymes down as the body is secreting them and it doesn't have to secrete them again."

That will seem like hard advice for most people, but Bob insists the rewards are worth it: "I just had my annual physical and my statistics are the best they have been in fifteen years. That's enough incentive right there! You know, the greatest cost any nation faces is the cost of aging and supporting people as they get older and fatter. My objective is to be as inexpensive for society as I can by being healthy for as long as I can."

Bob looks ten to fifteen years younger than he is and he produces so much energy that it is hard to remember he is 70. Clearly his health program works. On top of his obvious good health, Bob always dresses well and is always neatly groomed. He believes that it's not enough to just be successful, you have to look successful as well:

If you want to be the part, act and dress the part

"When you're dealing with the public," says Bob, "you're on stage all the time, but especially in the first moments. First impressions last a long, long time. People like to hang out with people they perceive as successful and they make visual judgments about success. One of my early mentors told me that the first thing he did when he graduated was to buy a Cadillac, buy two expensive suits, and only smoke expensive cigars. He started with nothing and died in the 1980s with a mid eight-figure estate. Not bad for a country boy who lived in Missouri. John T. Malloy's book *Dress for Success* is still, in my opinion, the best book on creating great first impressions through the way you dress. When people are well dressed they always feel better about themselves and transmit much more positive energy."

••

Clothes make the man. Naked people have
little or no influence on society.
Mark Twain

••

"Acting the part is also important," Bob adds. "One good example is that you should never get drunk in public. You have to be disciplined. I mean look at the impact of Michael Phelps smoking a marijuana pipe in public. It'll cost him millions. He might be young, but he should've known better."

••

Act like you expect to get into the end zone.
Joe Paterno, head football coach of
Pennsylvania State University, holds the
record for the most Bowl victories in history

••

Wade Micoley strongly acknowledges Bob's influence through this Lesson: "This statement has helped me in so many ways. If we are not growing and expanding, especially in this economic environment, we are dying, so we all need to get out of the psychological and physical boxes we place ourselves in. Bob has taught me that you cannot get to the next level without mentally placing yourself there first. You project yourself into the part before you are there and you create your new reality. Also, when I first met Bob I was impressed that he always dressed for success. Dressing the part is important because we are on stage to perform, to be the best we can be, so you will be remembered by people within a few seconds of meeting them. You stand a much better chance of winning their respect and trust if you are dressed for the game."
"You need to be conscious of the effect of everything you do," says Bob. "That includes the way you speak, your manners and how you relate to everyone around you. It also applies to your professional standards whether its in sales, investments, or day-to-day business.

Bob's Lesson here is:

You need a minimum standard for everything you do

"My standards grew out of watching other people compromise, then lose or fail. They didn't set standards for themselves. I can give you a great example of that. About four years ago I turned down thirty-seven consecutive real estate listings because either the sellers wanted too much money for them, or they weren't strongly motivated enough. In other words, they didn't really have to sell the properties. After I turned down the thirty-seventh one, I realized that for about three weeks I'd turned down every listing I had a chance to take. I said to myself, 'Bohlen, are you absolutely crazy? You can't create inventory if you keep turning down these listings.' One year later I looked back and thirty-six of those properties were still on the market! That's all about having a standard and in this case the standard was they had to be within 3% of the market or I couldn't afford to market them. The problem wasn't me, it was that the sellers weren't willing to price the properties at a level that would sell. If I had been willing to compromise and say, 'Well, it's only 10% over the market and maybe they'll adjust the price,' I would have taken all those listings and worked hard on them. I'd have blown about $75,000 because each time I take a listing it costs about $2000 in time, effort, marketing dollars, etc. just to get it on the market."

Mark Herman agrees with Bob about setting standards:

"Having a minimum standard means that if it is not challenging or significant enough, maybe it's not worth doing. I think that if you don't define your standards, you won't reach them. Also, if you haven't defined your standards, you're probably not sure what it is that you want to accomplish. Remember earlier when I talked about losing weight? If you say, 'I want to be healthier, I'm going to run.' That's a kind of general guideline: health by running. But if you say you want to lose ten pounds of weight within sixty days, and you are going to run a minimum of three times a week for twenty minutes, that's setting a standard."

Tomorrow we will look at how you communicate with others, but for now let's look again at today's Lessons:

- 🎬 **If you are not stretching both your mind and body, they are shrinking**
- 🎬 **If you want to be the part, act and dress the part**
- 🎬 **You need a minimum standard for everything you do**

Tomorrow's tasks:

By now you will know that fumbling through each day and just taking on tasks as they occur to you doesn't generate impressive results. Even worse, putting off things that need to be done doesn't generate any results at all! That's why it is important to get tomorrow's list down each day before you go to sleep…and don't forget to think about how long you are going to be sleeping. Sleep is important, but are you overdoing it? Or are you getting too little sleep? Sleeping too much or too little is one of the surest ways to interfere with how effectively you can use the time that is available to you

Tomorrow you need to get some independent advice about your appearance. Don't be afraid to go into a barber shop or hairdressing salon and ask for advice. If you don't know a good place to buy clothes, look at your friends or colleagues and choose one who you think looks great. Ask them where they shop. It's part of the process of self-education and there are people all around you who will respond with great advice if you pay them the compliment of asking their opinion.

If you don't do it already, you need to get your health checked. The best way to stay healthy is to eat well and regularly exercise. As we already know, the best way to make sure you exercise is to be Daily Accountable, so if you can afford a personal trainer it will help immensely. If you can't afford that, you can take out membership of a gym, or perhaps you can join a local walking group. The possibilities are endless and once you start you will quickly see the benefits.

These are not vague ideas. As Mark Herman said, 'health by running' is just a general guideline. You need to set goals for yourself to a certain standard. Decide what you can do to start this process tomorrow and *write it down now!*

PHASE THREE

Putting the Program into Practice

DAY FIFTEEN
Getting down to business

Until now many of the Lessons have been aimed at improving your general approach to life, either personal or professional. Although all of Bob's Lessons can be applied to most aspects of your life, from now on you will find the Lessons are increasingly aimed at your professional life.

Today's first Lesson has the double benefit of helping you gather all the information you need to make informed decisions, as well as leaving those you are talking to feeling good about themselves and impressed with how much you know. Sounds unlikely? Bob has no hesitation when he says this Lesson is one of the most important you will learn:

Always just ask questions and you will never get into trouble

Bob doesn't wait. After greeting somebody he always starts the conversation by asking a direct question. "Asking questions always helps you learn what you want to know," he said. "The skill is in asking the right questions and it's amazing how people are willing to tell you anything if you do that. I'm not sure any scientists would agree with me, but I've always believed that when most people are talking, they're convinced they're listening! Somehow, and I've seen this thousands of times, when people are answering your questions, they believe you are talking to them. Just last week I got on the plane and sat next to a crusty old guy. Before the plane took off I knew where he was from, how long he'd lived there, and who else in his family lived there. I even knew what his favorite restaurants were. I learned who he worked for and that he'd been to Japan 25 times, and he told me he was just coming back from Japan. And you know he didn't know a thing about me!"

My greatest strength as a consultant is to be
ignorant and ask a few questions.
Peter Drucker

"Once you start asking questions, people will feel you are interested in them or care about them. Then they feel totally different about you. People never forget how you make them feel. In contrast, every time you make statements, or judge something, you can get in trouble. If you ask questions – *and just ask questions* – you'll never get in trouble. You'll just get all the answers. When I do that with clients they'll often end a meeting by saying they've never met anybody who knows as much about real estate as me. And all I've done is asked questions and haven't made a single statement about real estate!"

Bob uses this approach every time when he is dealing with real estate clients. "Here's how it works," he says:

Bob Bohlen: "Do you want to sell?"

Client: "I suppose I do."

"Where are you moving to?"

"Probably to San Francisco."

"When do you need to be there?"

"Around next July."

"What did you pay for your home when you bought it?"

"$550 thousand."

"When did you buy it?"

"Nearly 12 years ago."

"What capital improvements have you made to the home and what did they cost?"

"I added two rooms and a deck. It all cost me around $50,000."

"If someone walked in the front door this afternoon what price would you be willing to accept for your property?"

"Hmmmm. $800,000?"

"Did you have an opportunity to review my listing proposal and package?"

"Yes I did."

"Do you feel I am qualified to handle this transaction for you?"

"It certainly seems so."

"Are you ready to put me to work for you?"

"You know Bob, I think I am!"

With absolute conviction Bob states: "This method has been the basis for a great deal of my success in real estate. By asking questions like these, without a single statement, I've successfully listed thousands and thousands of properties, whereas the average agent won't list 100 and probably not even 50 in an entire career. It's done just by asking questions and it generally it takes less than 10–15 minutes."

··

When people talk, listen completely.
Most people never listen.
Ernest Hemingway, American
Nobel prize-winning author

··

Bob stresses that this method works just as effectively in many kinds of business. "For example," he says, "it might be 'What kind of return are you looking for? What degree of safety do you want to have in your investments? How long do you want to be in the same investment? Are you interested in trading stocks on a regular basis? Are you a short-term player or a long-term player.' With cars would it be 'Is it a family car?,' or 'Do you go on long trips or mostly short hauls?' Every salesperson should be able to work out the right questions if they know their end point."

This leads to the next Lesson that is really the other half of *Always just ask questions.* It's a Lesson that most of us can quickly relate to because we've all had moments when we wish we could take back what we just said:

Don't editorialize, it will get you into trouble every time

"It's why people get into trouble when they make statements," says Bob. "You can't establish credibility just by making statements or promises. People just won't believe you because they are used to everyone telling fibs! That's why third-party references from people you have done business with are so effective. If somebody hears about you from another person who they respect and trust, you automatically obtain a mantle of respectability that you can never create for yourself. I've seen associates and competitors make presentations that took up to three hours, all full of statements, bragging, and impossible promises, but when somebody else says something good about you, it's twenty times better. It took a while for me to learn this lesson, but it works everywhere, in business relationships, guy-girl relationships, and parent-children relationships."

"I never make judgmental statements if I can avoid it," says Bob. "My experience has been that if I say, 'That guy couldn't possibly do that!,' I'll be wrong because my frame of reference doesn't allow me to believe that anybody could do that. People have said that about me all my life. 'How could he make a million dollars in real estate commissions? How could he make ten million dollars? How could he make twenty million dollars in real estate commissions? How could he own all that property? It's not possible!' What they are saying is, 'I can't conceive how that could be done,' rather than learning how it could be done. They make statements, editorialize, and shut off the possibility that they will ever learn how it might be done."

Robert Matheson has this to say about asking questions and not editorializing: "I agree with Bob that if you make statements you can always get yourself into trouble. When I met Bob my listing presentations were very statement based. I used to sit and talk to people for an hour straight without asking any questions. Now I start with 'What can I do for you and how can I help you get to where you want to be?.' It takes so much less time than before and I find out straight away what I need to know. Also, because I'm asking questions, I am showing an interest in the client and not just talking about what I can offer."

Bob believes this is so important that he reinforces it with another Lesson:

Make fewer statements

What a simple and powerful tool this is. All you need to do is practice asking questions and people will tell you almost everything you want to know! Later we will learn some specific examples of how to put this into practice, but for now you can start thinking about it on a very simple level. Today's Lessons, which go hand-in-hand, are:

- **Always just ask questions and you will never get into trouble**
- **Don't editorialize, it will get you into trouble every time**
- **Make fewer statements**

Tomorrow's tasks:

On your to-do list, write down a reminder to practice *just asking questions*. Maybe you will be spending time with somebody you don't know a lot about. See how much you can learn about them by asking a few simple questions. The second task is to begin practicing keeping your opinion to yourself, or *not editorializing*. How hard this is will depend on your own personality. If you tend towards being opinion-ated, this will be a difficult task for you. Resist the temptation to comment on the answers, and you might be amazed by how much they respond.

On Day Nine you were asked you to score people you meet on the basis of how positive or negative they are. Now you should score yourself on how you conduct conversations. Give yourself a score of between 1 and 10 on how well you are able to maintain Bob's advice of just asking questions. Give yourself a similar score on how well you avoid the temp-tation to editorialize.

As with all the Lessons, if you have time before you apply these Lessons it is good to discuss them with your mentor and agree on a target score. Then you can negotiate your rewards and non rewards. If you see your mentor less often, these are additional Lessons you have the option of including in your weekly negotiated package.

DAY SIXTEEN
Reinforcing the lessons

Because today's Lessons support what you learned yesterday, let's remind ourselves:

- Always just ask questions and you will never get into trouble
- Don't editorialize. It will get you into trouble every time

Asking questions comes much more naturally if you are genuinely interested in the answers you get. Bob says that he can't overstate the importance of this, which is why he created this extra Lesson to reinforce the idea:

Always be into curiosity, never into judgment

"The impact of being into curiosity rather than judgment has had a profound effect on my career," Bob explained. "In my early years all of my presentations were statement-based, and even though my energy and knowledge still let me capture lots of business, people's eyes would eventually glaze over. Finally I figured out that every time I got into judgment I was wrong. I started to think about a better approach and eventually worked out four questions to ask myself before each presentation or meeting:

- I wonder what I am supposed to learn from this meeting?
- I wonder if I will like the people I am meeting?
- I wonder if I will be able to help them?
- I wonder if I will want to?

"By asking myself these simple questions," Bob explains, "I'm able to prepare myself for the meeting and shift my energy so that I won't make a batch of statements and get into judgment too soon. During the presentation I'll ask enough to find out the answers to those questions. Once I have the information I can identify those I don't like, those I can't help, and those I don't want to help. Then I can focus on those I can and want to help."

....

*There are no foolish questions, and no man becomes
a fool until he has stopped asking questions.*
Charles Proteus Steinmetz,
German-American electrical engineer

....

When I don't like somebody," says Bob, "I just don't work with them. That simple process alone radically reduces my time investment in low-return, high-aggravation projects. It allows me to surround myself with people I like, projects I can learn from, and limits me to people I can really help who will also appreciate it. When people show me they are positive and want to get something done, then I've got to figure out how to help them do that. We feed on each other's energy and that's what makes the process successful. In fact I don't worry about whether people can help me because I learned a long time ago that whatever energy you put out in the world, it comes back time and time and time again. If you are positive and you help people, people will be there to help you if you need it."

Bob tells a great story that shows how he started learning about being into curiosity, not judgment.

"Back in my early cattle days I managed a top Black Angus cattle-breeding farm in North Salem, NY. A farmer came around in an old truck and I when I looked at him I thought he might be capable of buying a $1,000 bull, so I took him to the $1,000 bull pens. He asked if we had anything better, so I showed him the $1,500 - $2,000 bull pen. He looked at what we had, then quietly asked if he could see the bulls we were planning on exhibiting at the major upcoming livestock fairs."

"I was thinking they'd be much too expensive for him, but I showed him the bulls at the show barn anyway. He said he really liked two of them and would I be willing to sell either of them? I was surprised, but told him I would be willing to sell them. I explained that he couldn't take them home in his truck because we wanted to show them at the upcoming fairs. He said maybe that would be OK. After spending an hour discussing the merits of each bull, I asked him if he would consider buying both. He said he would and in five minutes we negotiated a contract. He purchased a 50% interest in each of them for $150,000. This was in 1962," Bob said, "and that was a lot of money back then."

"Of course, part of the lesson," Bob explained, "is the old adage that you shouldn't judge a book by its cover. In this case I shouldn't have assumed that somebody in bib overalls and an old beat-up truck was only qualified to buy $1,000 bulls. Years later, after being handed the same lesson a few more times, I realized that if you ask enough questions, you will probably get all the answers you need. If you focus on curiosity, you don't make judgments about people or projects until you know enough to make an intelligent judgment. Of course, when we're young and brash, we think we know everything, but as we get older we get better at understanding what we don't know. Maturity comes as you learn that you don't know very much about life."

Mark Herman once again agrees with Bob about how important this Lesson is: "It applies in every area of our lives and

I'll give you a good example. I'm from a modest background and although I've had a fair amount of professional success, I was never really exposed to the art world. If you pushed him Bob would probably say 'Mark doesn't know squat about art.' I'd look at a Picasso and say 'I really don't get it,' or I'd look at a piece of art that went at an auction for $2 million and I'd say 'You've gotta be kidding me!' But now I've learned that was my judgment side. Once I got rid of that I started to meet some new people who do wonderful things in their lives and even though I don't always agree with their taste, I've started to understand why they have a reference point that I didn't understand before and now I even own some art."

All of this is supported by Bob's next Lesson:

Knowing what you don't know is better than thinking you know a lot

This might seem like common humility, but Bob says it is more than that. "If you know that you don't know everything, you'll be into curiosity all the time, so you'll be learning all the time. If you think you know it all, you'll be into judgment and you deflect all the opportunities to learn more about the process you're in. You switch off from what other people have to offer."

....

*It is impossible for a man to learn
what he thinks he already knows.*
Epictetus, Greek philosopher

....

Let's remind ourselves of these four questions:

- I wonder what I am supposed to learn from this meeting?
- I wonder if I will like the people I am meeting?

- I wonder if I will be able to help them?
- I wonder if I will want to?

Today's Lessons are designed to reinforce your ability to make every meeting more productive.

- 🎬 **Always be into curiosity, never into judgment**
- 🎬 **Knowing what you don't know is better than thinking you know a lot**

Tomorrow's tasks:

Tomorrow you need to build on the tasks you performed today when you just asked questions and avoided the temptation to offer your own opinions and pass judgment. This is such a powerful tool that it will change your life. Continue to keep notes on each encounter you have tomorrow and give yourself a score from 1 to 10 on how you did. If you managed to end a conversation without making any statements, give yourself a 10. For every statement you made, take off a point. It will quickly become clear how well you are applying these Lessons.

DAY SEVENTEEN
Hard-hitting advice

When outsiders see successful people like Bob and all they have achieved, they often make simplistic assumptions about how it has happened. Bob says, "A lot of people think there is a hidden reason or some magic to what I do. They think they only have to write a check to this trainer, or buy that system, and they will be an overwhelming success. The reality is *there isn't any magic pill*. Whatever your business, success comes with hard work."

....

Opportunity is missed by most people because it is dressed in overalls and looks like work.
Thomas A. Edison

....

Bob has made this one of his most powerful Lessons.

There are no magic pills

"Most people choose not to succeed because they think it's hard work. They say, 'If it isn't easy, I could never do it. I could never study to be an electrical engineer or run my own business.' They want to find the Magic Pill. Well I have news for them. There aren't any! But there are so many simple steps anyone can take that will add up to success. That's what most of my Lessons are. Most of them are very simple, but they add up to big results. Take the last few Lessons for example. Anybody can learn to just ask questions."

···

Success is a staircase, not a doorway.
Dottie Walters, author of *Never Underestimate
the Selling Power of a Woman*

···

"Of course," says Bob, "people don't like the idea of working all the time, but they don't have to. It's important to remember that you have to find a balance. You need to have a personal life as well as a business life. It's not hard work for its own sake and in fact if you follow the program, it's easy! That's why I come back to this Lesson all the time:

Everything you do should be done with a system

Bob has arranged his life to guarantee *repeatability*. He researches anything that is of interest to him, finds out the most efficient and effective way to do it, and then develops a system to ensure that, as far as it is possible, he can get the same results every time. Bob was forced to develop this idea early in his career. "I guess the first time I really understood the benefit of systems," he says, "was when I drew the short straw to go and run the meat packing plant when I was a young man. At that time the only thing I knew was how much I didn't know, which was hard because I needed to know a lot about the business to run it. It scares the hell out of you when you're doing a million dollars worth of sales a day and if your net margin swings five or ten percent, you may make $100,000 a day, or lose $100,000 a day. You'd better figure out what you need to know pretty quick, because if you don't you'll be bankrupt. So I had to develop a set of key indicators that included things like cash in the bank, overtime hours worked, sales each day, number of times the manufacturing line stopped, yield on the cattle we were buying, and whether we made or lost money on a given day. That was the information I needed to make intelligent decisions on how to make the facility more profitable, so that's how we developed the system for running the packing plant. I've followed through by doing that for every business I've ever owned."

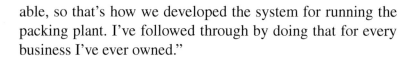

Success is neither magical nor mysterious.
Success is the natural consequence of consistently
applying the basic fundamentals.
Jim Rohn, business philosopher

"A lot of big businesses still haven't worked out these ideas because there's layer after layer after layer of people between the managers and the janitors. They might do fine when the economy is doing well, but when things get tough it shows up the flaws in the system. Look at the big auto manufacturers for example. The very first thing I always did when I bought a company was interview the janitor and work up, instead of interviewing the top executives and working down. The janitors always know what's going on. By the time it gets to the senior executives it's been filtered and refiltered three or four times."

Our best ideas come from clerks and stock-boys.
Sam Walton, founder of Walmart

Even after Bob explains how he does it, some people still believe that he is a special kind of person who has an extraordinary ability to analyze everything. "Maybe I can do that," he says, "but it's not that hard to put all the bits and pieces from your different experiences together into something that works. It helps that I do it every day, but it's also because I have an insatiable desire to learn and a lot of what I do is adapted from what other successful people have done. For example, I studied what Jack Welch has done at General Electric and what Hal Geneen did at IT&T. I take lots of little pieces and integrate them into the way I work. You really just need a program and the program I have developed works."

Because Michael Edlen, like Bob, had a different career in business before he became involved in real estate, he thinks very similarly. "A lot of real estate agents see themselves as involved in a sales process, but I see myself as involved in a business and to be successful it has to be highly systematized. In my office, if we have more than one or two steps to any process, it automatically becomes a checklist. If we have more than two checklists, it becomes, by definition, a system. We have checklists for property preparation, for photography, online uploading and maintenance of information on listings – the list goes on and on. That way, if someone is out of the office or on vacation, their work can easily be covered by someone else going down the checklists."

This brings us back to Bob's promise that you read at the start of the book and that he absolutely guarantees: the program he has developed *is foolproof if it is followed carefully.* "Sadly," says Bob, "most people don't want to be that accountable. People waste a lot of time and they're reluctant to face up to changing their behavior. I made a lot of mistakes and I had my head handed to me enough times to make it uncomfortable. I just wanted to avoid it happening again and now I know I can help other people avoid it too."

Over the coming days the Bohlen Program increasingly emphasizes efficiency in every aspect of your professional life. The key is to fully and consistently apply all of the Lessons and it has nothing to do with luck. Bob makes this clear with this Lesson:

Good luck is the result of preparation, planning, and seizing the opportunity

He explains as follows:

"People who don't have a plan don't have anything to work for, so they don't work much, even though they know they could be four or five times as productive if they did. As a result, they don't achieve as much. I like to say *the smarter and harder you work the luckier you will be*."

....

I've always been in the right place and time.
Of course, I steered myself there.
Bob Hope

....

Bob's long-time assistant Regina talks about how Bob pushes this message with his students:

"Five years ago Bob encouraged his students to learn all about foreclosed properties and how to negotiate short sales. Back then there were very few, if any. Many of his students went to seminars and training sessions to learn about this type of sale and now a high percentage of their business is listing and selling foreclosed or short-sale properties. By being ahead of the curve many were able to not only achieve their goals, but to exceed them."

Because Bob had predicted the '08 housing meltdown, he had re-targeted his business to compensate. "But it doesn't end there," he says. "I'm watching what happens to the US economy now and if it doesn't turn around we will have fifteen years like Japan went through after 1990 – stagflation and no GDP growth. I think there's a 50/50 chance that will happen. If that is the case, there are certain things we need to do to take advantage of that, including the kinds of assets you buy, kinds of tenants you have in buildings you buy or own, investments you make. If my analysis is right, new, small community banks are the best place to have your money, because the big banks' losses will continue, so their stock will have little or significantly reduced value."

Bob's approach seems very proactive in a time when most companies seem unsure of what direction to take. He makes his opinion about this kind of attitude quite clear. "They become paralyzed in victim mode saying 'woe is me!' Once they start saying that, nothing good is going to happen to them. They attract that kind of energy and sure enough, nothing good happens to them. I always plan on doing more. I always say *trying times are not the time to stop trying*."

....

> *Business opportunities are like buses,*
> *there's always another one coming.*
> Richard Branson, founder of over
> 360 Virgin companies

....

Today's Lessons are:

- **There are no magic pills**
- **Everything you do should be done with a system**
- **Good luck is the result of preparation, planning, and seizing the opportunity**

Tomorrow's tasks:

At the end of Day Ten you were asked to review the Lessons you had learned and revisit the Lessons that were most important for you. You were then asked to confirm your tasks and strategies with your mentor.

Now that you have learned so many more Lessons, tomorrow it will be time to repeat this review. Here is the task again:

1. Write down a new list of all the Lessons you have learned so far, then go through the list and underline those Lessons you think you have learned the most from.

2. If there are any Lessons that you have not yet acted on, or failed to follow up on as much as you think you should have, mark them with a large **X**. Make a separate list of those Lessons. Remember, don't avoid any just because you think they would be too much trouble. They are probably the Lessons you need the most!

3. Discuss these Lessons with your mentor. You need to identify the most important ones and negotiate your rewards and non rewards.

Constant review and revision are very important for your progress, so *give this task all the attention it deserves.*

DAY EIGHTEEN
Putting your business plan in writing

You've now travelled a significant portion of the journey that we promised you at the start of the book. Many of the Lessons you have learned are simple guidelines for daily life, but they all help build the foundations for success. If you have been adopting these strategies each day, you will already know that the Bohlen Program works and works really well.

The Lessons have included ways to help people you live and work with to appreciate you more, strategies to educate yourself for a better future, how to develop a life plan, understanding how to find out what you need to know by just asking questions, and many others.

On Day Two Bob gave you one of his most specific Lessons:

Goals have to be in writing or you won't achieve them.

It's such a deceptively simple strategy, that it is worthwhile repeating what Bob said:

"I have never seen anybody achieve anything they didn't write down."

Today you are going to see how this strategy applies to the business world and we will start with business plans because it builds on the goals you have already written down. "They're inseparable," says Bob. "Deciding on your goals is the first part of making a business plan. Then you have to put together the budget and plan for your time and money so that you see the goals are possible. You have to do it if you want to make your business a success. It's so important that I made it a separate Lesson:

If you don't have a written business plan you don't have a business

"You need to start with a mission statement, which is what you want to achieve in your life. One of my goals, for example, has always been to build independence income so that if I was not able to work for any reason, like health problems or an accident, I'd have enough passive income to maintain the lifestyle I want. Once you have decided what your life goals are, you need to analyze the economics of the business plan, what you need to create in net income each year and then, and this is important, what you are going to do with that income."

To prevent you losing sight of your goals in the day-to-day process of earning money, Bob offers a simple strategy:

"You need to look at your plan two or three times a day. That way it becomes a motivating force as you are frequently reminded that you are on track. There's really a push and a pull. When you are on-plan you feel good and you know you are accomplishing things. On the other hand, if you are off-plan it forces you to recognize that and then you can modify your behavior to get back on track. Also, once you move on, that original business plan will show you how much you have progressed. I remember when one of my colleagues joined our firm. She used to be a school-teacher and she was earning around $30,000 a year. In her first business plan she aimed for $36,000 a year. Ten years later, she was making between $350,000 and $400,000 a year. She never dreamed she could earn that much, so you need to remind yourself of what you have accomplished to stay positive and focused."

Bob also tells the story of a salesman he recently started working with:

"He's a super salesman who deals in oriental rugs. Unfortunately he was totally scattered in his approach. He needed to raise $250,000 capital to get where he needed to go, but he had no idea where to get it. Also he had a shipment of rugs worth $190,000 waiting in New York that he couldn't afford to pay for. We sat down together and developed a written plan for how he was going to make money on those carpets. Now he has a strategy to lease rugs to businesses. That makes a lot of sense because they can do that for one-tenth of what they would pay up-front to buy the rugs. Within forty-eight hours of writing down this plan, he had the $250,000 from other businessmen in town supporting his plan. They believed in him and his collateral, but most importantly they believed in his business plan enough to loan him the money. Without the plan he would not have even gotten to first base."

···

*The discipline of writing something down is
the first step toward making it happen.*
Lee Iacocca, American businessman

···

Bob's friend, software engineer Tom Droste, readily confirms what Bob says: "Bob got me to write out my business and life goals and I've found that 90% of the things that I write down happen within a year of writing them down. It gives you a mental shift when you write them down. It's like the difference between saying 'I should' and 'I will,' because you get what you focus on. It works for positive and negative things equally powerfully."

Many people think of writing a business plan as a boring obligation, perhaps something they have to endure for the sake of efficiency. In fact, the way Bob explains it, it is an inspirational act that you can perform for yourself. It is where you convert your dreams to concrete goals – and then to reality.

"It doesn't matter what you do," says Bob. "If you are a student working your way through college, an artist planning an exhibition, a person planning to buy a house – all of these people need to write down how they are going to reach their goals. It's as much a life plan as a business plan."

It might seem logical that once you have a business plan, you will need to develop yearly, monthly, weekly and then daily action plans based on the long-term plan. Bob's says that isn't true:

"You do need daily and weekly plans," he said, "but they don't grow out of your long-term plans. In fact they come first. They're the way you achieve the short-term efficiencies to help you achieve your long-term goals. Although you need to constantly look at your business plan to remind yourself of why you are working, you can't constantly assess progress for your long-term goals as too much time will pass before you succeed or fail. So you need to have short-term strategies that you can assess and be Accountable to. My Lesson for this is:

Having an Ideal Day and an Ideal Week
is the best way to maximize time management
and increase productivity

Bob explains further:

"By designing an ideal day and an ideal week, you can do the same thing every Monday, for example. It's about focusing on dollar productive activities. As I said before, just thinking about it won't work, but it's an amazing thing that writing them down seems to make them happen."

*It's not what you do once in a while, it's what you do
day in and day out that makes the difference.*

Jenny Craig, founder of the
Jenny Craig weight loss program

I'd say I achieve my ideal day nine out of ten days, but that takes discipline and that is one of the most important keys to success – the discipline to stick to what you have designed as your ideal days and weeks. For example, because I've recently moved from Brighton to Andover, I'm starting a new practice here, so I need to prospect on the phone looking for business, I need face-to-face appointments with prospective buyers and sellers, and I need to knock on doors. I know what I need to do to generate revenue and to get acceptance in this market place. It's what I call *back to basics*. That's where the ideal days and ideal weeks come in. They are absolutely essential if you are going to be effective."

Once again, here are the new Lessons:

- **If you don't have a written business plan you don't have a business**
- **Having an Ideal Day and an Ideal Week is the best way to maximize time management and increase productivity**

Tomorrow's tasks:

Tomorrow you need to begin discussing your business plan with your mentor. Think about what you are going to explain before you meet. You will find that explaining your ideas always clarifies them and a second opinion can help you avoid pitfalls. Don't worry too much about the timing of your business plan at this stage, we'll deal with that the next day. For now, look at the end goals, and give some consideration to how much money it will require to achieve it all.

At the end of this book under Appendix A you will find a form for outlining your Personal and Business plan. It's time to write your own plan. Even if the fine detail of that layout does not fit your personal circumstances, it is very easy to adapt it to your needs.

Appendix M contains a sample Daily Accountability form. Again, you can adapt this form to suit your individual circumstances.

DAY NINETEEN
Taking a long-term view

On Day Seventeen Bob explained how he had to learn how to develop a strategy to successfully run the meat packing plant. In the same way, he had to learn to plan ahead and avoid off-the-cuff decisions.

"Like everything," he says, "I learned the hard way and I'm still learning. Most people are more optimistic about what they can get done in a certain time than they can really do, but I've learned that you need to take a long-term view. In my business, for example, I've learned that if you buy a house, the odds are only about one in three that you will close on the day you expect."

···

Someone's sitting in the shade today because
someone planted a tree a long time ago.
Warren Buffet, American investor,
businessman and philanthropist

···

"Most sales people are optimists," Bob adds, "so we always think things are going to happen faster than they do. In fact that's true of most people. I'll give you a perfect example. I bought an office building in Fort Wayne, Indiana when it was 32% occupied. I thought we would have it filled up in two years, but it took us four. We did get there and we have added a lot of value to it by filling it up, but the Lesson I should have remembered is:

It always takes longer than you think,
no matter how long you think it will take

Perseverance is a recurring theme in Bob's life. He believes that life is a series of accomplishments, then reloading, and then another series of accomplishments. It is an approach to life that he learned very early:

"The greatest lesson I learned from my dad was that I could participate in any activity, but if I started I had to finish it. If I wanted to play basketball, I had to finish the season out whether I was playing or sitting on the bench. The message was 'never be a quitter.' When I was eight I was breaking a shorthorn steer named Pat to lead on the halter. He weighed 600–700 pounds, and I weighed maybe 65–70 pounds. Pat decided to take off and I hung on through the rosebushes, across the pasture, up and down the hills. I can still hear my mother saying 'Orlando! (my dad) Tell him to let go!' Dad simply replied 'He needs to get control of the steer. He'll be OK Virginia.' The only fight I ever heard my parents have was whether or not Dad should have told me to let go of that halter. I was covered with cuts and scratches from the rose bushes, but the steer finally stopped and I was still holding on. Dad told me how great a job I did and Mom screamed at him because I was all beat up and full of scratches."

"Sticking to it and never quitting has been important all my life. I've often seen others stop just short of success, but I've always seen challenges as opportunities and a reason to keep going, most times to a successful conclusion."

●●●

Consider the postage stamp: its usefulness consists
in the ability to stick to one thing till it gets there.
Josh Billings, 19th Century
American humorist and lecturer
●●●

"By the way," Bob adds, "Pat turned out to be the Grand Champion steer at the Shelby County Fair. Later he was third in his class of fifty at the Illinois state fair."

With this story in mind, it's not surprising that Bob's next Lesson is:

Perseverance is not a long race; it is many short races, one after another

"When most people decide they want to do something," explains Bob, "they might set a goal, but most of them get sidetracked almost before they get started. It's because their ultimate objective is just too far away, but if they can look at it in several stages, shorter steps in fact, it's going to seem much more achievable. If you want to travel around the world, for example, you don't just set out to circle the globe. You decide where you want to go first, say Hong Kong, and then plan the trip from there. Equally, you don't decide you want to make a million dollars until you learn how to make twenty-five thousand dollars, or fifty, or a hundred thousand. It's important to set long-term goals, but you achieve most of them in several short stages or you never get there."

••

You don't have to see the whole staircase,
just take the first step.
Dr. Martin Luther King Jr.

••

Mark Herman also sees any task as a series of smaller tasks: "If you are going to run a mile race," he says, "and you think of it in 100-yard, or quarter-mile increments, you'll probably finish the race. But if you come to the starting line and just take off, you'll sap your strength and after the first lap you wont be able to run any further."

- **It always takes longer than you think, no matter how long you think it will take**
- **Perseverance is not a long race; it is many short races, one after another**

Tomorrow's tasks:

It's time to refine your business plan by creating a timeline and setting intermediate goals. This process will not only make it easier to calculate the funding and logistics, it will reduce the big-picture plan to achievable stages.

Soon you will need to commit to your business plan, so once you think you have refined it enough to act on, you should negotiate the first of the short-term steps with your mentor. The rewards and non rewards for this stage of the Bohlen Plan need to be much more significant. By now both you and your mentor should be familiar enough with the process so you can decide what is achievable and what the appropriate incentives can be.

Now you should try this small exercise. Imagine you are undertaking this process without a mentor. Think about your plans and try to imagine what you would be doing tomorrow if you had not created your own system of Daily Accountability. How would you start your day? You might have a to-do list, but what would happen if you fail to act on it? Not much. How are you going to make sure that you keep your long-term goals in mind while completing the short-term tasks you need to make it happen? Your concentration will fail you eventually and you'll drift away from your plan.

Remember what Bob said on Day one: *"You have to have somebody to be daily accountable to. **You can not do it by yourself.**"*

DAY TWENTY
Friends and associates

On Day Eight you learned about eliminating negativity from your life. You also learned it can mean making hard choices about who you spend your time with. Today's Lessons look more closely at this part of your life.

Many times the people you do the most for appreciate it the least

"This often happens," Bob explains. "The people I do the very most for, either economically or by giving them exceptional service, sometimes don't particularly appreciate it. They certainly don't appreciate it as much as a lot of people I invest less energy in. It used to drive me crazy. Finally I accepted that the reality is what is important, not what they think it is."

"You need to learn that just because you do a lot for people they aren't necessarily going to appreciate it as much as you think they ought to. Some of the people I've done the most for just didn't know how to express appreciation. Maybe they were bought up in a family environment where you didn't thank anybody for anything. One of the easiest ways to tell how appreciative somebody is, is to travel with them and see how they treat the bellman and the doorman, and the waiters and waitresses. You can tell an awful lot about people that way."

This echoes the Lesson from Day Five about paying compliments. "All you have to do to make people aware that you appreciate them is to recognize them, call them by name, greet them with a smile, thank them when they do something for you, and ask how their day has been. It's not very complicated. These can be the people who can get things done that nobody else can do. I can go twenty-five hotels around the world and get tickets to the best plays, get a cab when I need one, things like that. It's because the people I've met there before really appreciate me appreciating them. It's as it should be."

This highlights how interdependent Bob's Lessons are, so it is not surprising that his next Lesson is the flipside of his earlier Lesson on eliminating negativity:

Associate with people who are better at what you do than you are

"I believe we shouldn't waste time with people who are negative. Also, you don't learn much from the people at the bottom of the pole. It's obvious that you learn more from people who are better than you are. When I was a young man in my first position after college I identified the smartest guy I could in the cattle business and six years later I went to work with him because it was clear I could learn more from him than anybody else in my field. That goes on all of our lives. There is always somebody better than us and the last person we worked with."

"One of the things I have my coaching students do each year is make a list of people they know, or people they have heard about who are better than they are, smarter than they are, or more successful than they are. They need to be people who are positive all the time. It's interesting that just by making the list several of them have lights go off in their heads. One guy looked at his list and said, 'You know, all of my old friends aren't very interesting to me any more. They all dwell on little stuff, and I want to look at and pursue the bigger picture.'"

It's better to hang out with people better than you.
Pick out associates whose behavior is better than
yours and you'll drift in that direction.
Warren Buffet, American investor,
businessman and philanthropist

Bob says his coaching students often tell him that their old high school friends just don't seem to have the same interests as they do any more. "They tell me that their friends are always saying, 'Well, why do you need to buy another car,' or 'Why do need to go to that event? Only snobs go there.' What's happening is that they are taking shots based on their frame of reference, not your new frame of reference. That's why I tell my coaching students to spend all their time with the people on their list."

Hitch your wagon to a star.
Ralph Waldo Emerson, essayist, philosopher, poet

At this point Bob emphasizes that outstanding achievers might not always be where you expect to find them: "I'm always finding people who are as good or better at their jobs than I am. It could be a janitor, it could be a bank officer, it could be anyone. The guy who does our landscape is a Portuguese man by the name of Johnny and he is as good at what he does as it's possible to be, so I have great respect for him. He takes a strong personal interest in the garden and grounds, and he has knowledge way beyond what I have in that area. It's about his pride and skill."

Again, Bob refers back to the earlier Lesson: "It all comes back to eliminating negativity from your life. That's why I tell my students *not to spend any time with people who aren't on the list.* As you start to succeed more, and it will happen really fast once you break away from the low achievers, there is always going to be some jealousy. The higher you fly the easier you are to shoot at, and the better you do the more people are jealous of you."

As you grow you will become a tall poppy. Most around you won't. Don't worry or feel guilty about leaving them behind

Mark Herman agrees with Bob on this point but he doesn't believe he has had to sacrifice the basic values that he thinks are so important: "A lot of my success has been because of the values that were instilled in me as a child. For example, my propensity to help others came from the way I was raised. But even though I come from a very modest background, my monetary success has allowed me to do some things that others can't. A good example is when my family took a three week trip to Africa. Some of my dearest friends could never do anything like that. My choice was either not to take the trip because they couldn't, or to take the trip and tell them about it and share the pictures when I got back. I have other friends who just have not been able to send their children to college. But that doesn't mean I'm not going to send my children to college. Certain things I might want to accomplish are going to be different than what my friends want, but I try not to judge them because of that."

••

Keep away from people who try to belittle your ambitions.
Small people always do that, but the really great
make you feel that you, too, can become great.
Mark Twain

••

In fact most people seem to fall somewhere between the two extremes of high achievement and under-achievement, but Bob explains that it is possible to insulate yourself from those who are just cruising by keeping this Lesson in mind:

If you don't expect much from your friends and associates, you won't be disappointed

He explains this as follows:

"I always see people's ability much more than they see it themselves. After working with thousands of people, I see that most have no limit to their talent, but most of them believe that their talent is very limited. I used to set extremely high expectations for the people I worked with and trained, but I was continually disappointed because they didn't show up, or they didn't do what they knew they needed to do to reach a certain level of achievement. It used to give me a lot of heartache because although I could see how much ability they had, they never lived up to that. Rather than continue to fight with myself over that, I decided that my job was not to determine how far people could go, but to show them the road and let them go as far as they wanted to, or chose to."

....

A true friend never gets in your way unless you happen to be going down.
Arnold H. Glasow, American author and
humorist who published his first book,
Glasow's Gloombusters, at age 92.

....

Today's Lessons are:

- **Many times the people you do the most for appreciate it the least**
- **Associate with people who are better at what you do than you are**
- **As you grow you will become a tall poppy. Most around you won't. Don't worry or feel guilty about leaving them behind**

■ If you don't expect much from your friends and associates, you won't be disappointed

Tomorrow's tasks:

Draw up a list of people you think are better at what you do than you are. Once you have completed the list, ask yourself why you believe they are better. If you really believe you can learn from them, it's time to find ways to associate with them more.

Make a second list of strategies to make this happen. Here are a few suggestions:

- Show an interest in how somebody you respect has achieved what they do. This is an example of Bob's powerful Lesson, *just ask questions*, at work. It will let them see you have a positive attitude and are willing to learn
- The ultimate expression of this strategy is asking someone to be your mentor
- Ask for a transfer in your job so you can work with high achievers
- Arrange social occasions such as dinners to deepen your connection with those you respect

It's important to develop your ability to think of your own strategies, so here is another suggestion:

- Look at the above strategies, then think of how to adapt them to your own circumstances. As Bob said in the introduction, it's not necessary to reinvent the wheel, but you do need to be able to adapt the Lessons to your own life. So a 'job transfer' for you might mean switching classes to a professor who you respect, or a 'dinner invitation' might become a good seat at a ball game. Work at it. As long as you are sincere, it will benefit you more than you can imagine.

PHASE FOUR

Business Matters

DAY TWENTY ONE
Getting the business

On Day Eighteen you read that Bob's Lessons would become increasingly more relevant to professional life. Because much of Bob's success has been in sales, many of his Lessons emphasize that aspect of business. But just as Bob's earlier Lessons apply to any aspect of life, the wisdom he has accumulated in sales and marketing is applicable to a wide range of business activities. The principles behind the Lessons are the same, so as you internalize the following Lessons you will be able to apply them to your own endeavors.

To show how this works, the first Lesson today is a repeat of what you learned on Day Seventeen. You will remember that Bob told us how most people look for the easy way to succeed in many aspects of their lives. Now that we are going to look closely at sales, Bob wants to repeat this basic Lesson:

In sales there are no magic pills

"The keys to success in sales," says Bob, "are prospecting, face-to-face appointments, asking questions, dealing with objections, and closing. They are all hard work and require development of the skills, but as I said before, following the program makes it easy! It always comes back to working on the basics."

The words "hard work" are enough to put off many people, but Bob thinks that is not important. "If people don't want to succeed they'll find excuses. But it's no good lying to people and promising something that won't work. The fact is that if you do the hard work there are great rewards. The really good news is that *it's possible and anybody can do it!*"

Bob starts with prospecting: "One of the most important ways to prospect is just getting on the phone, calling your data base and asking for business. It's pretty much the same for all salespeople, whether it's securities, insurance, or advertising. Another simple way is just handing out cards to people and asking them for the business, or asking people to refer the business to you. As a matter of fact, that simple action is one of the most effective prospecting methods of all. It's so effective it has its own Lesson:

Start each week with 25-30 business cards and hand them out to everyone you meet

"It's that easy to find new customers," said Bob. "Just hand out cards to people you meet and ask if they know anyone who is interested in buying or selling your product. One out of ten will yield a result. It doesn't matter if you are an electrician, an engineer, a computer software salesman, or an air-conditioning serviceman. Most people need one of these people at some stage and it might as well be you! If you give good service, your clients will give your card to their friends."

"There are other very simple ways to find new customers," says Bob. "You can just call the telephone book. One of the most successful agents I ever coached moved from Birmingham, Alabama, to San Francisco and didn't know a solitary soul there. The first year he was there he made a million dollars in commissions by simply starting with 'A' in the phone book and prospecting till he got to 'Z.' Then he went back to 'A.'"

Most people have received these calls and they can be irritating, so Bob stresses the importance of what he calls "telecasting the right kind of energy. If people believe you might be able to help them, or satisfy a need," he says, "they'll never hang up on you. Let's say you are calling Mr. Smith:

Mr. Smith, I'm a real estate agent down the street. Are you folks planning on moving in the next six months?
If he says *'no,'* you could say,
If you were going to move, where might you move to?
'I might move to San Francisco.'

Now you've engaged him.
Really? When would you like to get there?
I don't know, it's probably not practical right now.

You can build on the fact that you've engaged him by saying:
Mr. Smith, who else do you know who might be interested in buying or selling any real estate?

Because you said *Who else do you know?*, he'll stop and think about it. If you said, *Do you know anybody else?*, he'll probably say *No*. It's all in the linguistics. You need to engage the customer."

"The next Lesson is one I have to repeat to my students all the time because Daily Accountability depends on it. I've already told you that Daily Accountability is the most important Lesson of all, so this is also crucial:

A weekly top prospect list is crucial to your business success

Bob explains how this works:

"The Daily Accountability process forces people to review each day, whether or not it was productive. When income earners are at the level my program can help them achieve, being off track for a week or two is just unacceptable because it costs them tens of thousands of dollars. The program is designed to keep them laser sharp, on track, doing their prospecting, keeping in front of prospective buyers and sellers. I provide them with a form that they use to send me a weekly list of their top buyers and sellers. It's to make them focused. I also ask them to have it in their hands all the time so they don't forget to follow up and call somebody that they should just because they get unfocused or confused. They need to rank the prospects by the most income to them first, then rate them on a scale of one to ten for how likely they are to do something with them in the next thirty days. Then there's a slot in their form to put in when they last communicated with them. That allows me to tell whether or not they are staying on top of their top prospects. The rule is that if you have somebody who is going to buy something in the next two or three weeks, you need to be talking to them every day. It really prioritizes the people who can generate income and revenue."

Bob is convinced this works as well with businesses other than real estate, as he explains: "A weekly top prospect list is a list of the people you want to do business with no matter what industry you are in. You can only control the output by controlling your input. There is often a view in sales that you ought to measure your success by the closing commission income you generate, but if you focus on that closing commission income, you miss the whole point. What you have to do to get that income is to have face-to-face appointments with motivated buyers and sellers. To do that you either have to call them on the phone, follow up e-mail leads, or go out and knock on doors. That's the input! You have to do enough input to get the appointments so you can do the deals that result in the output. I like to compare it to a funnel that you put grapes in. You have to keep adding grapes on top and stomping on them to keep the wine coming out of the bottom. In the same way, you just have to continually keep adding prospects."

Today's Lessons are:

- **In sales there are no magic pills**
- **Start each week with 25-30 business cards and hand them out to everyone you meet**
- **A weekly top prospect list is crucial to your business success**

Tomorrow's tasks:

Your first task is very easy. If you don't already have a business card, get a batch printed. Don't try to be too clever with it as simple design with basic information is most effective. If you are going to be dealing with your clients face-to-face, it helps to have your photograph on the card. Bob explain, "What we have learned is that people rarely throw away a business card with a picture on it."

Make sure you have business cards with you at all times and, most importantly, *use them*! They are a primary prospecting tool.

Now you need to create your weekly top prospect list. Remember, this list is created by prioritizing leads according to potential income from them, how likely they are to do business, and when they last communicated with you. At the end of this book in Appendix K you will find a sample Top Prospect List that you can adapt to your needs.

Explain this process to your mentor and once you have generated your first list, lock in the process by making yourself Accountable. The process of doing this with your mentor should be automatic by now: discuss; agree; commit; negotiate rewards, non rewards and timeline; report back at agreed time.

DAY TWENTY TWO
Focusing even more

Yesterday Bob told us about the importance of prospecting. Today he will expand on this topic, giving us more important advice about this primary sales tool.

Bob has a simple rule of thumb:

P3 – Prospect, Prospect, Prospect, Q3 – Question, Question, Question, C3 – Close, Close, Close

"I treat a prospect just like a baseball player," he said. "Three strikes and they're out! If I try to call them three times and I don't get them, I don't call back. If I try to do business with them three times and don't get anywhere, I don't waste any more time. Generally I can tell in the first phone conversation if people are interested in doing business or not, and anybody can develop that skill with experience. The question and close part of the Lesson is how you deal with each prospect. You have to ask the questions to find out what they are interested in and how to create a deal that will work for them, then it will be that much easier to close the deal.

Bob's next Lesson is:

You can't qualify a prospect too much before meeting them

"Before you meet with somebody face-to-face, the more questions you ask them, what I call *pre-qualifying* them, the better it will be. Let's imagine I'm talking to a potential real-estate customer:

BB: *Do you guys absolutely want to buy a home.*
Client: *Well, really we're just kickin' tires.*
BB: *Let me make a suggestion. I'll put you on an e-mail list and if you find a property that you like, send me the information.*
Client: *I guess that's OK.*

Then, while I have their interest I ask a series of questions like this:

To be sure that I get you the right houses, how many bedrooms are you looking for? How many baths? What price range? What geographic area?

Finally I suggest:
Let me set up an appointment with one of our loan originators so we can get you pre-approved for a mortgage so you know exactly what you can afford. Does that make sense?

That's the end of the conversation. I quickly got all the information I need, but if I bring them in to my office it takes time out of my schedule. If they're not motivated that's a really low-yielding use of my time, because I need to be focused on working with people who are ready to do something. The same thing is true of car sales, or any other kind of sales where you are talking to people on the phone before you sit down with them."

Bob has a good example of how this works in real life: "I recently had a meeting where I signed a lease for a farm client of mine who lives in Europe. He's leasing his farm to some dairy farmers here in Michigan. Before they drove 45 minutes to come into the office to see me, I asked them all kinds of questions, such as:

What kind of crop year did you have last year?
What's your current financial position?
What do think milk prices are going to do?

On a scale of 1-10 how much do you want to lease this property? How much do you really want to pay for the lease?

There was more like that until I found out that they were motivated and really did want to lease the property. They came in at 1:30 and by 1:40 we'd signed the lease for 35% more than they'd offered. My client in Europe was tickled to death with that. If I'd not asked all those questions, when I sat down to meet with them I'd never have known whether they were motivated or not. If I didn't think I could get them to raise the amount they wanted to pay, I wouldn't have wasted my time with them. I was focused on the key information and the reason for that is another Lesson:

Knowledge is power

Bob explains that equipping yourself with the information you need before you negotiate with another person gives you a distinct advantage. "Look at what I told you on Day Nineteen about the Internet lead system and how much that has helped us anticipate a client's needs," says Bob. "This approach not only works in real estate, but it will work in almost any sales environment."

Once you change your mindset by using the four questions Bob told us about on Day Sixteen, you will be able to learn more, help people more, and you will enjoy better outcomes from your dealings with other people. Let's remind ourselves again of those key questions:

- I wonder what I will learn from this meeting?
- I wonder if I will like the people I am meeting?
- I wonder if I will be able to help them?
- I wonder if I will want to?

"By now it should be clear how all the Lessons work together to help you reach your objectives. I can't over-emphasize how important it is to *just ask questions*," says Bob. "It's really just doing your homework. You need to know exactly what you want to accomplish as well as what the other person wants, then you know what questions to ask. Once you are negotiating you can remain focused and as long as you keep smiling and remain positive, people will really respond and you will almost certainly finalize the deal. "

Today was really focused. Let's look again at these Lessons on prospecting:

- **P3 – Prospect, Prospect, Prospect, Q3 – Question, Question, Question, C3 – Close, Close, Close**
- **You can't qualify a prospect too much before meeting them**
- **Knowledge is power**

Tomorrow's tasks:

Draw up a new weekly top prospect list, but this time create a space for recording how often you have tried to contact each of them and/or how often you have spoken. This list will change more often than any other list you make except your daily to-do list, so you need to be sure you can track what you have done.

You need to develop your own presentation for qualifying customers. By combining previous Lessons and just asking questions, you can create a set of questions that will bring you all the information you need to close the deal to everyone's satisfaction. A script will allow you be consistent and you will have a known process to fine-tune as you get better at it. You will learn more about this tomorrow, but for now start making notes of your ideas to make this work.

DAY TWENTY THREE
Closing the sale

Over the last two days you have heard from Bob how important prospecting is and how he converts leads into information that will help him create a deal that the client will accept. Once you've learned as much as you can about what motivates a client, it's time to meet with them face-to-face to negotiate. Once more, you will be able to use all of the Lessons you have learned, but *Always Just Ask Questions* will be your most important tool. To help you focus on this even more, Bob offers this new Lesson:

Start your presentation with the end in mind

Bob explains that the questions you ask in your sales presentation should have a very simple purpose – to find out exactly where the customer wants to end up:

"If you are selling autos, it will be questions like, 'How long do you expect to have the car?' or 'How many miles do you think you'll put on it annually?' because that will determine whether the customer leases or buys the car. If you are selling insurance, you could ask 'Where do you want to end up five years from now?' The detail will vary, but the principle behind the questions remains the same. Determine exactly what you need to know to close the sale, then frame the questions to gain that information."

"That's how it works in real estate," Bob says. "If you have a property that you are thinking about selling, unless I can find out what you are going to do with the money when you sell it, *I'll never get to the point of selling it*. By *starting with the end in mind*, I mean that you take people to the end and work backwards. So I ask questions like:

Are you sure you really want to sell this property?
Where are you going to move to when you sell it?
When do you see yourself in there?
What kind of price range are you going to be moving into if you sell the property?
When do you really need to move?
Can you see yourself relocating without your family, or do you want your family to go with you?

As long as you know where you are heading with the questions, they will make sense."

Bob continues: "It's also very important to keep in mind that you are closing on the deal the whole time. My Lesson here is as simple as:

ABC

"That stands for *Always Be In Control and Always Be Closing*. It means you always need to be asking for the business, and that means you need to ask questions that bring you closer to closing the deal. It's always about asking questions and here is how it works:

BB: *"Did you have a chance to review my presentation?"*
Client: *"Yes I did."*
BB: *"Do you feel I'm qualified to handle the transaction for you?"*
Client: *"Probably."*
"What are you looking for in an agent?"
"I want somebody who is really aggressive."
"Do you feel I'll be aggressive enough for you?"
"Well, yes, I'm pretty sure you will be."
"What's the best experience you've ever had with an agent?"
"Um, the guy who sold my last house really seemed to care about keeping me informed."

"Is great customer service really important to you?"
"Yes it is."
"If I can give you great customer service, are you ready to put me to work for you?"

It's hard for anybody to say 'no' to that question after the build-up. So the answer is almost certainly going to be...

"Yes."

"You see, I've closed five times and it hardly felt like it. I'm just taking what the client said and asking the questions back. My job is to determine what they want. It might seem that closing once is enough, but it's been shown in study after study that before people buy something they say 'no' to buying it seven times. 95 – 97% of sales people in the world never ask people to buy something enough times. The Lesson is:

Ninety percent of the people won't proceed until you've closed them seven times

"That's why 4 or 5% of us do most of the business," Bob says. "It's because we go beyond that threshold and ask for the order seven or more times and because we deal so thoroughly with any possible objections. I also believe that *too many sales people don't ask for the business."*

•••

*If you don't go after what you want, you'll never
have it. If you don't ask, the answer is always no. If you
don't step forward, you're always in the same place.*
Nora Roberts, best selling novelist with
over 280 million books in print

•••

Tom Droste confirms that Bob's prospecting and sales strategies are just as effective for his software engineering company. "These were very hard for me," he says. "Until I understood Bob's approach, I would call two or three times and then give up. Now that I never give up I have found that sometimes *even after twenty rejections I get a yes*! Just recently I got a meeting with a prospect I had been calling once a week for 6 months. During all that time they had never returned one phone call. You have to be that persistent."

So Bob's belief is that closing is a whole sequence of questions aimed at obtaining one positive reply after another till the client is committed to finalizing the deal. It's because most people try to resist answering too positively and they often try to preserve at least the appearance of resistance. "That's why you have to frame your questions so they always answer 'yes.' It's because:

If it is not YES it is always NO!

"To get the answer that you want you may have to give the other person some things to help them feel good about the outcome. Any deal has to be good for both parties. But you always have to look for an unequivocal 'yes' before you proceed, and if you don't get it, you don't have a deal. It's human nature to try to avoid being pinned down in discussions like this, especially if it is a big decision. I'll give you a great example. One of the most difficult things I have to do is to get my students to commit to being daily accountable. If I say:

'Do you really want to be daily accountable?'
They might say,
'Well, it's really hard for me because sometimes I don't come into the office till 10:00, and I just can't figure out how to get my daily facts to you by 2:00.'

What they are really saying is they don't want to be daily accountable enough, and that means they don't understand the benefits of it. It's up to me to get them to agree that they understand the benefits and get an unqualified 'yes' about that before I proceed to asking them if they really want to do it. I believe that communicating with people is like peeling back the layers of an onion until you get to its heart. You've just got to keep peeling till you get the answer you need."

....

Remember, you only have to succeed the last time.
Brian Tracy, author and sales coach

....

"This applies just as much to daily life as it does to business," says Bob. "People give indirect answers all the time. If you say to your wife, 'Do you want to go and see a concert this evening?,' and she says, 'Could I get back to you on that?,' what she's really saying is 'No, I don't want to go.' She qualifies it because maybe she doesn't want to hurt your feelings, or she may want to consider her options. But if she really wanted to go she'd say 'yes'!"

Robert Matheson finds that although people are reluctant to give a straight "no", if they don't say "yes", then there must be a reason and that is the time to dig deeper and find out why. "For example", he says, "if someone doesn't like a home that I show them, it may be because they wanted extra garage space, or another bathroom. I have to find out what it is standing in the way so I can show them something else until I get a 'yes.' Unless I get that 'yes,' we're not doing business."

Doug Ferguson thinks that following up a qualified answer with more questions assists the buyer as much as the seller: "It helps them clear up their thinking," he says. "It's a clarifying process for both the person asking the question and the person giving the answer."

Today's Lessons are:

- **Start your presentation with the end in mind**
- **Always be closing**
- **Ninety percent of the people won't proceed until you've closed them seven times**
- **If it is not YES it is always NO!**

Tomorrow's tasks:

Now you have the information to begin refining your sales presentations. A script should be based on known successful strategies, so yours will depend to some extent on what business you are engaged in. It will not be too difficult to find material that is specific to your industry, but it is important to remember that all scripts should be question-based.

Your script will become one of your most important tools. You need to be able to adjust your script according to the results it brings you. It also has to be something that you follow comfortably and that you can adapt to individual client's needs. You need to practice your presentations for qualifying and closing, so your to-do list should include contacting as many prospects as you can to put your new script into action.

DAY TWENTY FOUR
Making sure the client feels good about the deal

Yesterday's Lessons were about closing the deal. Today we'll learn more about making sure the client is comfortable with the process. "If you try to push a buyer or seller to take a particular offer, you risk them rebelling on you," Bob says. "If you feel like you *have to* have something happen, if you are emotionally attached to the transaction because you have to have the fee or the commission, that's when it never happens. But if you can shift your head away from the outcome, people can read that. If you say, 'I really don't mind if you take the deal or not, but in my opinion it is the best offer you are going to get and you need to think about the consequences if you choose not to take the offer. Whatever you decide is OK with me,' it totally shifts the relationship."

This is a very important Lesson because you can destroy a lot of hard work at this late stage by giving the wrong message to the client. It's no good having the best weekly top prospect list in the world if you put the client off by trying too hard. Bob's Lesson here is:

The more detached you get from the outcome, generally the more attached it gets to you

Bob explains further:

"What you are offering may be a great deal, but if you try too hard it can become a competition to see who prevails and the client will question your motives. If you quit pushing and just ask questions, you can find out what motivation the seller has and in the process you get detached from the outcome. Usually people think you're only interested in collecting the fee, irrespective of what is happening to them. This is particularly true in a market where prices have gone off 10 or 15%. If that happens all you have to do is step back and let them see that whether they accept the offer or not is not going to affect your lifestyle. When they see that, they start thinking about how it affects them rather than worrying about how it affects you."

It may be hard to stand back from what you hope will happen, particularly if you have worked hard to reach that point. "But," says Bob, "you have to learn to do it. As a real-life example, I just finished advising a long-time client about buying a restaurant. He was in the process of liquidating some assets, but he knew that he couldn't meet the deadline and there was another offer on the restaurant. He was really worried about what to do, but I told him he was worrying about something that he had no control over. It would either go through or not, but if he agonized over it he'd fall in a hole and get depressed. I told him to liquidate the assets on the assumption that the other offer would fall apart. If it did fall apart, he would have the cash and wouldn't need to borrow to do the deal. If the other offer went through, he could find something better to do with his cash. It turned out exactly as I thought it would and he got the restaurant, but if it had gone the other way he would still have been ahead. When we started, he was about to become too attached to the outcome and all I had to do was show him that it wasn't that important."

Bob always keeps in mind that buying or selling a house is an emotional experience for many people. "If somebody has an emotional commitment to a deal, it doesn't help to work with them in an emotional way. You need to be logical and business-like to help them through that process. Most people understand that the relationship between a client and a sales agent is based on what's in it for the other person, not necessarily what's in it for them. It's a Lesson we need to keep in mind:

People only care about *what's in it for me*

"Once you show them they can get what they want and it doesn't make a lot of difference to you, you are that much closer to a deal. That's why it's important to have a good top prospect list. When you have a only a few clients, you are going to be more dependent on the outcome and that affects how you deal with them. But if you have twenty or thirty prospective clients and one or two fall through, you won't care so much and you will be able to be more detached. That will be reflected in how you do business with all your clients and it applies to all business"

....

It is not from the benevolence of the butcher,
the brewer, or the baker that we expect our dinner,
but from their regard to their own interest.
Adam Smith, 18th Century, known as
the father of modern economics

....

"One of the reasons clients don't trust salespeople is that too many of them are ready to promise anything to get the deal. People have had their fingers burned and they don't want it to happen again. I always get a lot of repeat business and that's because I always bring more to the client than they expect. My Lesson is:

Under promise, over deliver

"Perception is everything. If a basketball coach says he can win ten games and he wins twelve, fans will think he's far better than if he said he was going to win thirteen and won twelve. *The result is the same in both cases, but the perception is totally different."*

"It's the same for everybody. If I predict that something will sell for, say, $20,000 and it sells for $25,000, that'll be an exciting result for the seller. On the other hand, if I say it will sell for $25,000 and it sells for $20,000, even if that was a great result the seller will be disappointed. You always need to be able to deliver more than you commit to deliver and that means that in a presentation you under promise so you can over deliver. The customer will always remember what you said you can do. If you fall short they won't think very highly of you, but if you exceed what you said, they'll think, 'He's really good at what he does!'"

* *

When my mother had to get dinner for 8 she'd
just make enough for 16 and only serve half.
Gracie Allen, American comedienne

* *

Once again, Michael Edlen agrees 100%. "Over the years," he says, "I've learned how crucial it is to manage your clients' expectations. Many people try to please everyone and in the process the clients develop very high expectations. If those expectations aren't met, they won't be very pleased. It's just as easy to promise 90% of what you can do and then you're a hero if you deliver 100%. Also, it's not just about money. I noticed a while back that if somebody called for information and my staff told them we'd call them back shortly, people were expecting that they'd receive a call within 15 or 20 minutes. If they got a call 2 hours later with the information, people weren't pleased because they didn't think that was 'shortly.' We now say that we'll get back with the information within a couple of hours. If we call them back within 30 minutes, we've under promised and over delivered!"

Today's Lessons are:

- **The more detached you get from the outcome, generally the more attached it gets to you**
- **People only care about *what's in it for me***
- **Under promise, over deliver**

Tomorrow's tasks:

At this stage in the program you should be busier every day because you are more focused on particular goals and you are managing your time more carefully.

Instead of a new task, tomorrow you need once more to re-assess how successfully you are putting the Lessons into practice. Also, you should work your way back through the *Tomorrow's tasks* of all the previous days. This is because any uncompleted task will hold back your progress. They have been designed to focus your attention on every day's Lessons and to help you internalize what Bob has to teach.

When you have completed this task, take the time to get feedback from your mentor and affirm once more your commitment to the Program.

DAY TWENTY FIVE
Selling is about price, price and price

You have less than a week to go till you complete the Bohlen Program. Over the last two days you have learned about ways to help you finalize a sales negotiation. Today we will hear what Bob has to say about advertising in sales. His first Lesson may be a surprise:

If you price a product right, it will sell quickly with little or no advertising

"It's not difficult to understand," says Bob. "You can sell anything in the world, anytime, if you price it right. It doesn't matter what you are selling, the same Lesson applies. The opposite is equally true. Lots of advertising or marketing will never get an overpriced product sold."

"Of course some products are more suitable for advertising than others. It helps to understand that there are basically two kinds of sales. One is shorter cycle and the other is longer cycle. Retail sales such as drugs, food, cosmetics, cars, and appliances are all examples of shorter cycle sales. If you go into a supermarket and pick something off the shelf, that's instant, or if you buy a washer or dryer, you buy it on the spot. Advertising in these areas tends to be much more successful."

"Longer cycle sales are in areas such as service contracts, software contracts, security and life insurance sales, real estate, and so on. These are the kinds of things you don't buy the minute you see them. You think about it, compare prices, analyze the monthly payments, return on investment, and so on. It's a sale with a much longer relationship between the customer and the agent. Some agents are more suited to relationship sales and others are better at shorter cycles. Assertiveness and aggression are much higher with people suited to retail sales. It has to do with their impatience and ego. The principles behind sales in both areas are the same, but there are people who are better at one or the other."

Bob gives a simple example from his own industry: "If I list your house for $300,000 and it's worth $200,000, I can spend millions of dollars advertising it and nobody is going to buy it. If I price it at $199,900, I might get three or four offers on it and I'll sell it very quickly. People already know roughly what a house should be worth. In fact, these days they know what most things should be worth. The Internet has made it easy for people to find the best prices for anything. Today if somebody wants to buy a computer, they don't just go to the nearest store and buy what the salesperson offers them. They check on the Internet and find the best price."

It seems that a lot of advertising money must be going to waste. Bob is sure that is true: "What we learned years ago in the real estate industry has really been proven true in the last few years. You can spend a lot of money on advertising, but you never get the results back. In my whole career I've not spent much money on advertising that ever got me a return. You can *never* measure print advertising results. We haven't advertised in a newspaper for nearly twenty years and our market share has grown for every one of those years. My Lesson here is based on a lot of experience:

Most sales people spend way too much money on marketing and advertising

"In fact," says Bob, "a lot of advertising is for the salesperson's ego. I've been told by some people that they spend 12-15% of their gross income on marketing, but I can tell you that we don't spend one hundredth of one percent on marketing and personal promotion! Of course that means more goes to the bottom line. In sales, most advertising doesn't do much for anybody. We have a trainer here in the United States who's promoted personal marketing and advertising for the last 25 years. Lots and lots of agents who follow that trainer go broke because they spend more on advertising than they take in. They don't treat it as a business, don't hold the spending accountable and don't focus on results."

Let advertisers spend the same amount of money improving their product that they do on advertising and they wouldn't have to advertise it.
Will Rogers, American cowboy,
humorist and social commentator

Bob tells a wonderful story about his early days when he started the first Gelato Classico store outside of California, in Scottsdale Arizona. "I thought the product was great and if people would just come and try it, it would be a huge success, so we distributed 200,000 flyers with coupons that entitled the bearer to a free cup of ice cream worth $2.95. All they had to do was show up and present the coupon. Here's an amazing thing. Scottsdale is a small area and the store was right on Scottsdale Rd, but only 147 coupons out of 200,000 came back! It had no measurable impact on the store's activity."

"It was a big waste of time and money, so we hired 25 high school kids at $5 an hour and gave them all the ice cream they could eat to stand around the store from 6:00 to 10:00 in the evening eating ice cream and talking. Within one week the store was packed every night and it stayed packed for as long as we owned it. It cost a lot less than the flyers and we got a fantastic result. All those coupons went for nothing. Even really good mailing firms will tell you that a return as low as 1 or 2% is fantastic. That's why you have to be careful about what you spend your marketing budget on. If it is accountable, you can simply apply the numbers. For example, if you spend $2000 on advertising, you should decide what you need to get in return. It can be $6000, or $10,000, but you need to be getting a return. In my opinion, if it is not trackable, you are wasting your money. You'll never know whether it had an impact."

"But," Bob adds, "the good news is that in today's world things are trackable. For example, the pay-for-click process on the internet is working well. The difference is that you can measure it every day. Successful advertising is the combination of a whole lot of things, but, as I repeat all the time, if most sales people would only prospect, the business would come and their bottom line would be substantially better."

Rick Ferris agrees with Bob that you can waste a lot of money on advertising. "I spend virtually nothing on newspapers, absolutely nothing on magazines, and zero on personal promotion. I do spend a little bit on the internet where I can track every result and of course I can track the results from our own website on a daily basis. In fact we've eliminated most of our advertising because I don't think it brings results."

If you do decide to reduce your advertising budget, you need to be sure that you have the right strategies in place to maintain business growth, as Bob explains: "Some people build their businesses during good times out of referrals and business from past customers and clients. That often means they do the same things over and over. It also happens with people as they get older because they quit looking for new business. My next Lesson should shock them out of their box and get them to do something different:

If more than 25% of your business is repeat and referral you aren't growing your business enough

This reflects what Bob said on Day Three about welcoming change. He admits that it's not always easy to find new ways of doing something you have been doing well for many years, "But it's always possible! For example, I never stop looking for new ways of finding leads and a year ago I discovered an Internet-based lead system. It has revolutionized how I do business and now my coaching students who are using that system are getting 80 – 90% of their new leads that way. What's more, they're getting up to 500 a month! You know, if we had been satisfied with business the way it was a year ago, we wouldn't be getting 80% of the new business we have now."

• •

If you have always done it that way, it is probably wrong.
Charles Kettering, holder of over 300 patents
including the electric starter motor

• •

"It's a simple system," says Bob. "Because people register their details when they use our site to look for property, we know how often they're on the site, how long they spend on it, exactly what properties they're looking at, where they are looking for a property, and what the price range is.

With that information we're better equipped to satisfy their needs. When we know how often they've been to our site and what they are searching for, we know whether they're a hot prospect, or a *really* hot prospect. You can start building a relationship with them straight away. It's a lot of work, but in sales it's the wave of the future. If you get 400 leads a month and some of them come back 2 or 3 times, you can be dealing with 1100 contacts! If you do what you are supposed to do to get business from them, either you have to talk to them, or e-mail them and then follow it up. If you don't do that, nothing ever happens."

Doing all that work, however, has it's rewards: "For each 100 inquiries," explains Bob, "20 register phony names or phone numbers. Out of the 80 left, we are getting between 8 and 10 face-to-face appointments, which is 8-10%. Of those, we are closing 35%. It's amazing! The return is between $9 and $12 back for every dollar spent and, best of all, it's a lot better than any other advertising medium because you can hold it 'Daily Accountable'!

Today's Lessons are good examples of how Bob's advice is often simple common sense. They are the kind of Lesson that you can easily remember and easily apply:

- **If you price a product right, it will sell quickly with little or no advertising**
- **Most sales people spend way too much money on marketing and advertising**
- **If more than 25% of your business is repeat and referral you aren't growing your business enough**

Tomorrow's task:
If you advertise your business, you need to assess the effectiveness of what you are spending money on. Is the marketing

you are doing trackable and can you assess its effectiveness? Can it be held accountable? Do you know what the return is on money spent? You need to set up a system for assessing these factors. As Bob says, simply apply the numbers. If you don't know whether the money you are spending money is working for you, you are probably better off cutting this expense from your budget.

DAY TWENTY SIX
Customer Service makes the difference

Bob Bohlen's success has not been limited to boom times. In the past and during more recent market fluctuations, he has continued to prosper when times are tough. Partly this is due to his anticipation of market trends and early preparation for a changing market, but it is also due to the fact that his company provides such good service that his competitors find it hard to keep up. It's a key part of his successful strategies and his Lesson is:

We're in the service business and our goal must be to provide great service

Always open to new ways of doing business, Bob has continually adapted to changing times. "Twenty years ago when I listed a property I was able to just tell somebody that the next time they would hear from me was when I got an offer on it. That worked pretty well at that time. Pretty soon though, people started going to Disney World and they started staying at the Four Seasons, or they started working with Fedex. From all of these organizations they learned about customer service. We weren't getting that kind of competition from other agents, but people were starting to have higher expectations and we needed to provide that kind of service to this industry."

"Great service means you are customer-centric. That means you are focused on what the customer needs, not on what you may *think* they need, or on what you need. It's simply understanding your client's needs, and that means asking lots of questions, which most people don't do. As I say again and again, most people talk all the time, but you need to listen a lot and understand what the customer's needs are, then try to respond with the kind of service that will satisfy them."

· ·

Customer service doesn't come from a manual, it comes from the heart. When you're taking care of the customer, you can never do too much.
Debbie Fields, founder of Mrs. Fields
Bakeries and best-selling author

· ·

In his business dealing with commercial properties, Rick Ferris believes he offers services that clients don't get elsewhere and that makes it much more likely they will return to him with future business: "For example, I always offer my clients help with the tax implications of investment in commercial property. If I think I can save them money I always suggest ways to do it. I'll talk to their attorney and their accountant as well if they need it. When I'm doing a lease for someone, I'll always try to find out what their future needs might be. They might appreciate an option to expand or contract, to terminate or buy. These are all things that they may never have thought of. A few years ago I spoke to some clients about purchasing a building. They hadn't even thought about it, but a couple of years later they made $500,000 on the deal! It makes you feel great if you can help someone in a way they never even knew about. I can't imagine ever feeling that I had done everything I could. There's always something else to offer clients."

Bob highlights one of the main failings in sales: *"For years salespeople have been doing **sell and tell** rather than **ask and provide**.* Everybody in sales needs to understand this next Lesson:

Mind-blowing customer service is the wave of the future in sales

"If you buy a house from us, you get free use of one of our moving trucks. When you arrive at the house the day you move in you will find a care package of cleaning supplies, paper towels, and a vase full of flowers welcoming you to your new house. At noon on the day you move in somebody delivers two pizzas to the house so you don't have to go out and find food. That's real service," says Bob, "and it could work for someone who is selling cars, or anything else. They could learn from what Lillian does. She has the details of every client she has ever worked with and she keeps track of all their kid's birthdays. On those days she sends them a birthday card and a McDonald's gift certificate."

"People always appreciate what you do for their kids more than what you do for them. It's the kind of message that stands out. There are other ways to make your message stand out. For example, I send 4th July cards and Easter cards, but not Christmas cards. That's because everybody gets lots of Christmas cards. When I send a card I want them to recognize the card is from me and that I am different from all the other people sending them cards."

Bob goes further and says that charity work is a kind of service too. "As a community service," he says, "our salespeople, assistants, management, and support staff work together on a monthly charity. Last year, for example, they collected 1/2 ton of groceries and several hundred dollars for the St. Louis Center, a caring residential community in Chelsea for people with developmental disabilities. Agents helped by driving the truck to and from the site as well as helping collect the food and unloading it after the event. A month later, we collected 837 lbs of food and several hundred dollars in Fowlerville for the Family Impact Center. We help Gleaners, the Salvation Army – lots of good causes. That's another important use for our trucks. We believe that if we work in a community, we need to show everybody we are willing to support the community."

Bob thinks that many salespeople have the wrong idea about service. "A lot of other agents take a proposal to a prospective customer, then work with the customer to help them decide if they want them to be their representative. I do it in reverse. I bring the sellers in and let them feel they are interviewing me. They get to see the environment I work in and how our systems function, so then they can decide whether or not they want to hire me. If they do, I go to work. Of course, in reality I'm interviewing them and I can determine how motivated they are."

"It's simple really and I keep coming back to this, usually I'm the only one who ever asks the questions and I find out all that I need to know before we proceed. I can't tell you how many times I've asked twenty or so questions in around fifteen minutes, and then the customers have got up to leave and said, 'You know, we've never met anybody who knows more about real estate than you do!' People believe what they tell us, not the other way around. It's really, really important," says Bob. "Clients don't need us to tell them what we want. Their needs have to come first:

> **Our customers and clients
> only want four things from us:**
> **a. Time**
> **b. Knowledge**
> **c. Negotiating Skills**
> **d. Attention to their needs**

"Negotiating isn't only about getting what you want for or from the client," says Bob. "I can give a great example and again it's based on that really important Lesson, *Just ask questions*. When I'm interviewing a prospective client, I always ask them how many other agents they have interviewed. If they have interviewed other agents, I ask, *'Why didn't you hire one of them?'* Let me tell you, the answer to that question tells you what you need to do to if you really want the deal to go through but, and here is the great part, it is also *exactly what the client wants!* It always comes down to asking questions and it can benefit the client as much as you."

"These Lessons apply to any negotiation. Next time you're trying to get somebody to agree to something, just find out what they want first and I'll guarantee you can get a result that everybody is happy with. If something does go wrong, if you do have a dissatisfied customer, it's really, really, important to fix the person first. But to make sure that the person is fixed you have to resolve the problem – and to do that you have to listen to the person!"

When a customer feels their service has been unsatisfactory, fix the person, fix the problem, fix the system

"It doesn't make a difference whether you are talking about checking into a hotel or buying a new car, the rules are the same," says Bob. "When you fix the system, the mistake won't occur again. The ability to convert upset customers into lifetime customers is almost guaranteed if you follow this process. People get irate for lot's of reasons. Maybe the new freezer they ordered wasn't delivered when they were told it would be. Maybe they thought that the person buying their house was going to take it as is, then they find the buyer wants the gutters fixed. It might be as simple as a customer in a restaurant getting mad because the food was cold when it arrived at their table."

"It goes like this:

Angry customer: *I thought you said my refrigerator would be delivered today and it hasn't happened. What are you going to do about it?*

BB: *I don't have absolute control over the delivery truck. Let me ask you, if we can get the delivery done tomorrow and give you a $50 gift certificate for the delay, would that be an acceptable resolution for you?*

Can you guarantee you can do that?

I'll do my very best. Is that what you would like for me to do?

OK, that's good.

"When most people get mad, they're not mad at the person they are talking to, they're mad at themselves because they didn't control the situation before it occurred. If you give them back the feeling that they have some control, they are more likely to be satisfied."

Wade Micoley has this to say about fixing the problem: "I've heard Bob say many times, 'Bore into it, get to the core of it!' He's always looking to see what the real challenge is, to cut through the blame game, through the hide-your-head-in-the-sand. Whether you run a big organization, or just a one-person business, things are going to go wrong. They always do. The fun part is tweaking and fixing things to run as well as they can. If there is a problem, there is only one proper thing to do and that's to *fix the problem*. It's your business, it's your career, it's your responsibility, no one else's. Once you accept that fixing the problem will never be finished, your organization will continues to improve, problem by problem, challenge by challenge."

If you are about to embark on a business career, the last few days have taught you the most important things you need to know about customers' needs. Today's four Lessons are an action plan for better customer service and you need to start putting them in place tomorrow:

- **We're in the service business and our goal must be to provide great service**
- **Mind-blowing customer service is the wave of the future in sales**
- **Our customers and clients only want 4 things from us: Time, Knowledge, Negotiating Skills, Attention to their needs**
- **When dealing with an irate, fix the person, fix the problem, fix the system**

Tomorrows' tasks:

Bob makes it clear that in business the most important people you deal with are your customers. You need to look at how you are dealing with them. Are you offering the best service you can? Is there some service you can offer that will give an edge over your opposition? How do you deal with unhappy customers?

List the services you provide and ask yourself if you can do better. Write down ten new ideas for offering better service. It doesn't matter if they seem unrealistic because at this stage you are only stimulating new ideas.

When the list is complete, think them through again and then select the best three. Take these ideas to the people you work with and brainstorm ways to make them better.

Most importantly, *act on these ideas.*

DAY TWENTY SEVEN
Using your time productively

Bob firmly believes that once you start earning the kinds of commissions that are possible, there are many ways you can use your newly found financial independence to further enhance your earning power. It's time to look at how you earn your money and ask yourself if you are using your time effectively. Bob's first Lesson is:

Track any lead that comes in, cost it, and
quit doing anything that isn't profitable
by a ratio of four to one

On Day Twenty Six we saw how most marketing people spend too much on advertising, this Lesson refines the process even further and allows you to identify precisely whether you are using your advertising dollars effectively.

"We record the source of every call that comes into my office," says Bob. "As I said before, we don't advertise much, but if we are spending marketing dollars, we expect to get at least four dollars back for every dollar we spend. The only way you can do that is track your calls, track your sales, your closings, and your commissions against the sources so you know where you are spending your marketing money effectively. I'm effectively holding our advertising dollars totally accountable, which is the same as holding people accountable."

Bob emphasizes this dollar accountability as follows: "A person should always focus on dollar productive activities. In real estate it's *Prospect, List, Negotiate, Sell*. In mortgage origination it's *Prospect, Take Applications, Get Loan Approvals*. If I'm a loan originator, I take your application, then

I hand it off to somebody who does all the paperwork, puts it in the computer, and follows up the process. That way I'm free to get out in front of another person who wants a loan. It should be true of all sales people because they're almost never detail-oriented. They don't make money by doing paperwork or getting bogged down in detail. If they're not in front of a buyer or seller, or on the phone negotiating a sale, they need to be prospecting for candidates. We hire people at a lower rate to handle the details and every area in business should be the same."

When measuring productivity is so important, you'd expect Bob to have a system, and he does: "For years we've had people use a stopwatch to record the time when they are actually engaged in prospecting, listing, negotiating, and selling. Amazingly, what we continually find is that most people only work an hour or less a day on dollar productive activities. Most people don't even work ten minutes a day! It's incredible that most people will come into the office, work all day, then go home and tell their significant other that they are exhausted from working hard all day, when in fact they only worked for less than an hour at things that will make them money. But it happens every day. People stand around the coffee machine and gossip about all the negative things that are going on in the world instead of doing what they are there to do. If you are capable of earning thousands of dollars an hour, why should you do things that you can hire somebody else to do for twelve dollars an hour? It's a simple Lesson:

Delegate everything that is not dollar productive

"The ratio I've worked out over the years is that if you can hire somebody to do something for you at one-fourth of your hourly rate, that will free you up to do what you do best. Delegation makes total sense. I always say, *if you don't have a personal assistant, you are one*. If you are doing all the other stuff, you can't focus on the things that make you the money. Every sales person or executive does things that make them more money than other things."

For those who don't feel they earn enough to do this, Bob has good news: "Once you start to follow all the other Lessons, the point where you start to earn enough to delegate comes very quickly and it immediately creates a huge jump in your productivity curve. Sales people generally *hate* details, so if you can have somebody handle the details for you, you will be happier in your job, you will be doing what you are best at, and you will be far more productive. It's better if you are out meeting people, asking questions and taking orders, while somebody who likes dealing with the details is sweeping up behind you."

....

Why should I clutter my mind with general information when I have men around me who can supply any knowledge I need?
Henry Ford

....

"It's easy to do," says Bob. "You just set a cost level and anything below that level, you get someone else to do. You don't want an executive who is generating a major portion of the company income working on something that somebody else can do cheaply. I'll give you a good example. Our presence on the Internet is really important for our business, but we can hire people to design web pages and put information on the Net for $10 to $15 an hour. It doesn't make sense for our top sales people to spend their time doing it."

This basic arithmetic gives us one of Bob's simpler Lessons:

**If you can find someone that will do
something at a 1/4 of your hourly rate,
hire them and give them the task**

Bob explains why so many people don't follow this common sense idea: "Most marketing people never figure out what their income is per hour. Here's a simple example: if somebody works 2000 hours a year and makes $200,000 a year in commissions, that's $100 an hour. So getting somebody else to do the laundry and rake the driveway at $12 per hour is better then doing it for themselves at $100 per hour. You have to like raking the driveway an awful lot to invest $100 an hour doing it! The same principle applies to any task you can identify."

Doug Ferguson believes that people you hire to work for you at lower rates of payment can benefit in unexpected ways. "They'll end up with a whole lot more expertise in that area than you can ever have and although they may bring in less dollars per hour than you do, that will make them an important link in the chain and they can build their career from there. Just because somebody is paid less, doesn't mean they aren't important. If you think of a brain surgeon versus a podiatrist, one of them is going to be paid a whole lot more money, but both of them are absolutely needed."

Today's Lessons are:

- Track any lead that comes in, cost it, and quit doing anything that isn't profitable by a ratio of four to one
- Delegate everything that is not dollar productive
- If you can find someone that will do something at a 1/4 or 1/5 of your hourly rate, hire them and give them the task

Tomorrow's tasks:

Your next task is to set up a system for checking whether you personally are spending your time and dollars effectively.

Firstly, make a list of things you do that somebody else might be able to do more cheaply. This list could include household duties like washing the car, fixing the fence, and so on. At work it can include any part of your job that is eating into your more productive activities. One way you can identify these tasks is to keep a daily log of everything that you do during the day and then separate those activities into 'productive' and 'non-productive.'

Your second task is to use the same activity log to identify tasks that you can delegate to people you work with. As Bob says, it can be because they are not dollar-productive activities, or it can be because it is a task that is not suited to the kind of person you are.

Finally, if you are able to track costs for your leads or other direct income-generating activity, apply Bob's simple rule: if it isn't profitable by a ratio of four to one, *quit doing it*! This last strategy can be difficult to apply because businesses often continue with unprofitable work for many reasons, such as loyalty to long-term customers, unwillingness to change, or even because they have not sat down and calculated whether it is worth doing. But if you want to maximize your earning power, *you have to do it*!

PHASE FIVE

Taking the Lead

DAY TWENTY EIGHT
Finding team members

Bob's Lessons have become more focused and specific as you develop your skills, increasingly targeting specific strategies to benefit your professional life. Whatever your business, if you follow these Lessons carefully, you will find yourself taking a leadership role much quicker than you thought possible. It's time to start thinking about how you are going to manage those who look to you for guidance.

Remember way back on Day Four when you learned that *what you do should be fun every day*? Bob Bohlen is surrounded by people who clearly enjoy what they are doing and he feels this is a key to further success. He explains that the process of developing a working atmosphere like this starts even before you hire staff. "The process of managing people is so much easier if you hire the right people in the first place. Most companies create a job description, set a compensation range, and then try to find somebody to fit in the compensation range. What they should do is find the best person and then figure out how to pay them. In that sense you select people, you don't just hire them. It's so expensive to hire and train people, then lose them or have to fire them because they don't make it. Every time you have to let somebody go, or somebody doesn't make it, you've got to start the process all over again. From a management perspective it's the greatest loss of time and energy. Employee turnover is the most costly thing in running a business, so it's always better to hire somebody who is the best person for the job and then figure out how to pay them."

The most important thing you can do as a leader is hire the right people

"You don't just throw out an ad on the Internet saying 'I have a job position that I want to fill' and then sit back and wait for the applicants to come in. Don't wait! You look at a particular position and then go through all of the people that you think might best fill that position. That means you select them. If you encounter really great people, then hire them."

....

The best executive is one who has sense enough
to pick good people to do what he wants done,
and self-restraint enough to keep from meddling
with them while they do it.
Theodore Roosevelt

....

"I'm always looking for people who are positive, smart and well presented. They should want to make money and be committed to learning and growing. There are so many people over the years I've worked with that I encountered in another environment doing a great job, but it only happens because I'm always looking. I have a Lesson for that too:

Adding team members is a never-ending job and potential candidates are everywhere if you just look

Bob has found that team members can be found in the most unexpected places: "I've hired several waiters and waitresses because they had great customer service skills," he says. "Some went on to make it and some didn't. A good example of how this can happen was when Lillian and I were flying to San Francisco and we met a flight attendant who really impressed us. She was very gregarious, smart as a whip, and already owned some income properties with her husband. I asked her if she had ever considered a career in real estate and she said she had. Because she lives near our office, I asked her to come in so we could see if she wanted to work with us. Things went really well, so she took a real estate course and got her license the next month. A week ago she wrote her first offer and her share of the commission on that first offer is $6,000."

It seems surprising that people with no previous link to a particular industry can be so suitable, and Bob agrees that it is sometimes helpful if you already know people, or if they know how you work. "Past customers and clients make great team members because you've already had a chance to work with them and learn if they are positive or negative, and what their energy level is. Also, if you did a great job for them, they know that you expect anybody on your team to do a great job for the people they work with. The standards are set higher with past customers and clients than with anybody else because they've encountered the services you've provided."

Mark Herman personally verifies this: "That's how Bob employed me", he says. "I met Bob when I was relocating to Brighton Michigan. I called a close friend who lived there and told him I needed a broker to help me buy a house. My friend said, 'There's this guy named Bob Bohlen and he's phenomenal! Just do what he suggests and he'll be wonderful for you.' I met Bob and we had a half-hour conversation, which I thought was normal. I didn't realize that getting an uninterrupted half-hour of Bob's time is almost unheard of and that Bob did it because I had been introduced by our mutual friend. So I bought my first, second and third houses through Bob. I've also referred hundreds of clients to him over the last 15 years. As time passed our relationship grew and one day he said to me, 'When you grow up what do you want to do? I don't think you want to be a banker all your life.' He was right, so I left a very successful banking career and came over to run Anyi Management for Bob. Since then it's been phenomenal."

Mark says the broader message is that as you deal with people, you can build friendships and learn more about their talents. "In the business world many of the things that you are skilled at can translate to different types of businesses. It might have been easy for some people to stereotype me as just a general banker because they wouldn't know that I'd had several very different roles all over the country, including working in different geographies, different business units, that I had specialty training in many areas, some sales, some management, some finance. Bob was able to recognize that. So if you build a personal rapport with somebody, or solved some problems for them over a period of time, they might appreciate you enough to help you as well."

Interestingly, because Bob leaves the question of salary open, it might seem that would lead to higher costs, but he doesn't think this is necessarily the case. "The money you pay people," he says, is not the only reason why they might want to work for you. Other things are more important to many people, which is what my next Lesson is about:

Compensation is generally fifth on the list of what employees want most in their job

Bob explains that studies by many prestigious institutions, such as MIT, Harvard and others, have generally found that compensation is the fifth most important thing to an employee. "The first thing on most people's list ," he says, "is whether they are appreciated. As we discussed right at the start of the book, you should let employees know how good they are.

The second thing on people's list is whether they're challenged, because most people want to go on learning.

Third is if they like and respect the people they are working with. I know that's the case with us.

Fourth is whether they like the facilities and environment they are working in. We've created an environment with around 130 pieces of original art, granite floors, and tall ceilings. It's an open, airy environment that our employees love.

Only then, fifth, is whether they are compensated enough. I have lots of people who stay because they are really appreciated. We do pay competitive or above-competitive rates, but even if they could make more money someplace else, that's not the most important thing for them."

Bob knows these things are true because he is surrounded by people who prove it. "If you can satisfy all of these criteria, people stay longer and work better. Today I had lunch with my assistant Regina, my CPA and tax attorney Harvey, my chief financial officer Larry, and Mark Herman. Harvey has worked for me for 40 years, Larry has worked for me for 35 years, Regina for 20 years, and Mark and I have been associated for 12 years. Obviously they are happy with what they are doing and I'm satisfied with their performance, or it wouldn't have lasted so long."

An important part of selecting and incorporating new employees into a team is recognizing and utilizing their strengths. Bob has a great tool for helping him decide who is suitable for a position.

People are either operations people or sales people

Yesterday Bob talked about how sales people don't like details, and here he explains how easy it is to find out this kind of detail about potential employees: "Herb Greenberg designed a psychological testing system called *Caliper*. It's his theory that people are either operations people or sales people. In my experience, he's right. I've given hundreds of these tests to people and it's really evident that people who score high on ego, assertiveness, aggressiveness and motivation, and who score low on attention to detail are salespeople. People who have high attention to detail and low ego, etc., are operations and accounting people. So *I always Caliper prospective associates and employees.* When I interview someone, I have their Caliper profile in front of me and it works every time. After years of tracking this process, I can tell you the results are very consistent. Out of every 32 interviews we do, we select 4 candidates to do Caliper tests. Out of those 4, we will hire 2. From those 2, only 1 will make it for 5 years or more."

Again, Mark Herman confirms what Bob says:

"Bob would consider me an operations person," he said, "and I think that although I've had a lot of sales experience it's true. We're polar opposites. Bob's an extreme sales person and I'm an extreme operations person. One of the things Bob does every day is clear his desk. Everything either goes to another person, or into the garbage. Part of the stuff that goes in the garbage probably shouldn't, but he believes that he's read it, processed it and given it to somebody else. He says, 'I'm done with it, what's next?' I tend to say, 'I'm glad you gave that to me because we have to pay those bills and we have to do a report for the bank.' Bob believes that's what my role is and that he has delegated the task. Bob is right, people tend to have a personality type, and their education and professional training usually reinforces those things."

Today's Lessons to help you become a better employer are:

- **The most important thing you can do as a leader is hire the right people**
- **Adding team members is a never-ending job and potential candidates are everywhere if you just look**

- **Compensation is generally 5th on the list of what employees want most in a job**
- **People are either operations people or sales people**

Tomorrow's tasks:

At the end of this book under Appendix L you will find information on how to access the Caliper test. You need to start using this powerful tool, firstly to ensure you employ people with the attributes you need, and secondly to ensure that people you already employ are working at what they are suited for. Perhaps the most interesting beginning to this process will be to Caliper yourself!

Your second task is to review your employment practices. If you are following the standard 'advertise and hope' method of finding new employees, it's time to become more proactive.

DAY TWENTY NINE
Managing others

Managing a team is one of the biggest challenges you can face. How are you going to make sure they all perform as well as they can and produce the kind or results they are capable of? Bob has several Lessons to guide you and the first is:

Building great teams requires high-energy teamwork

"You need to put people in situations that challenge them," Bob says. "You praise them when they respond and you also praise them when they succeed. In many office environments, particularly sales offices, when somebody else succeeds they'll find negative things to say. The higher you fly, the easier you are to shoot at. It's important to get rid of that attitude. We have meetings five days a week and we encourage everybody to ask questions and help each other deal with problems. We also hold annual award nights where people's achievements are formally recognized and prizes are given. They're great team-building exercises and everybody feels like they belong."

••

Individual commitment to a group effort –
that is what makes a team work.
Vince Lombardi, legendary football coach

••

"It not only develops great loyalty," says Bob, but it also develops great performance. I've never had a sales person leave any organization I was with and do as well at the next organization. A while back three really good agents left us when we reorganized. Recently I got their results for the past year. One of them was at 10% of what he'd produced the year before with us, another was 30%, and the other was 32%."

To explain how he has achieved his amazing results, Bob describes why many teams don't work:

The number one reason people are unhappy at work is that they don't know what is expected of them

"Not only don't people know what is expected of them," he says, "but when they do a good job, nobody tells them they have done a good job. Nobody appreciates it. This is another example of how Daily Accountability is the most important Lesson of all. To make sure people know what is expected of them, they have to report to me every day, so they know if they are meeting or exceeding targets, or not. I always try to hand out meaningful compliments to people in the normal course of business and if people get the compliments, they know they are appreciated and they are doing a good job. On the other hand, I might say 'Next time why don't we do it this way and it might work out better for us than the way you did it last time.' This extends down the chain of responsibility because I set the standards of direct supervisors and insist they have a daily accountability system in place. This system permeates all of the organizations I'm involved in. Because anybody who works with me sees that I put it into practice every day, they know I'm committed to it and that it works."

....

*Good leadership consists of showing average people
how to do the work of superior people.*
John D. Rockefeller, American
industrialist and philanthropist

....

Bob sum up his strategy for managing people as follows:

a) **Set expectations**
b) **Hold them accountable**
c) **Give them feedback regularly**

"My employees look to me for energy, motivation, leadership, creative thinking, attacking problems outside the box," Bob says. "The Lesson is:

All employees want leadership and the best leadership is by example

"Everyone who works for me knows the door is always open. They know that I really care about them, and that I'll give them the best advice I can. All top producers have big egos. Most of the time they should be able to figure out how to solve their difficulties, but they want the attention and recognition from a higher-up to help them sooth their ego. So I give them that attention."

It might seem that the need for attention conflicts with the need to make employees self-reliant, but Bob says this isn't the case: "If you give them the encouragement, they need less and less attention. Also, although I try to give positive messages, they also know I'll tell them what they need to hear, even if it's not what they want to hear. It's like the age-old adage, do you feed people fish, or do you teach them how to fish? If you don't force people to think through potential solutions to the problems they have, they just keep coming to you for the answers. If they come to you with two or three solutions and you help them pick the best one, they learn from thinking through how to solve the problem. Not only do they grow, it also makes your job much easier. You might not be able to think of a solution, but if they've thought of two or three they must have really thought about it already. You can use your experience to help them choose."

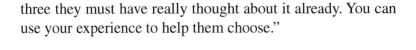

Pull the string, and it will follow wherever you wish.
Push it, and it will go nowhere at all.

Dwight D. Eisenhower

Doug Ferguson likes to be a good example on many levels: "I don't just reinforce the business lessons that I think are important. I think it works on all levels. For example, I also try to dress better and present a better image as a role model for them."

Wade Micoley adds: "Bob has always shown me about leadership through his own actions. If the leadership chain is broken or weakened, it will transfer to the customers you serve and will destroy your plans for long-term success. People need leadership, sometimes without even knowing it. They want a person with a vision and Bob has done this for so many people, in so many areas of life."

Of course, none of this means that Bob won't step in if things go wrong, as he explains: "People who are not leaders stand back and criticize or affix blame. Often all they want is to avoid being blamed themselves. It destroys morale and generally it doesn't get the problem fixed. Great leaders jump in and fix the problem quickly. Mediocre leaders only tinker with things that are going right and eventually screw them up. They don't address the things that are going wrong. My Lesson here is:

A real leader spends time fixing the problem
instead of finding who to blame

Bob believes people who are really changers are:

a) Leaders
b) Proactive not reactive
c) Don't hold on to the way "we've always done it."

....

The best job goes to the person who can get it done
without passing the buck or coming back with excuses.
Napoleon Hill, author of *Think and Grow Rich*,
one of the best-selling books of all time

....

Again, Doug Ferguson wholeheartedly agrees with Bob: "I always tell my staff that it doesn't matter how many mistakes they make. The important thing is not the mistake, it's the recovery. I tell them to *always save the client*."

Today Lessons in Leadership are:

- **Building great teams requires high-energy teamwork**
- **The number one reason people are unhappy at work is that they don't know what is expected of them**
- **All employees want leadership and the best leadership is by example**
- **A real leader spends time fixing the problem instead of finding who to blame**

Today's tasks:
If you find yourself in the role of team leader, you may already be aware of the responsibilities and challenges that brings. However, as we have repeated throughout this book, it is always valuable to step back and reassess what you are doing.

If you are not already in such a role, being prepared with these Lessons will equip you to make the most of future opportunities.

Tomorrow's task is simple because at this level you are already capable of assimilating and acting on new strategies: review the Lessons on leadership and act on them where you can.

DAY THIRTY
Coaching

Today is the final day of the Bohlen Program and you have been learning from a great master of business practice and life skills. It is the next best thing to being personally coached by Bob Bohlen and it is time to remind you of what you were promised at the very start of the book.

"You *can* change the way you live and work. If you follow Bob Bohlen's program *you will realize your dreams*."

Now that you have some idea of how Bob coaches other people, this final day's Lessons will give you more detailed insight into how coaching works. If you follow Bob's Program closely, eventually others will look to you not only for leadership, but you will be asked to mentor those who want to emulate your success. Bob's Lesson is:

Your life's job at this level is
to be a coach to others

Bob explains this as follows:

"I think that if an industry or a business has been good to you, then you are obligated to give back to the people in that industry to make it better for others coming behind you. I really enjoy all of my coaching and I think that's because I keep in mind that I'm not just a coach. A good coach is a psycho-analyst, a psychologist, a mentor and a trainer. By incorporating all of these things into what I do, every week I can offer new challenges for the people I work with and it keeps it interesting for me as well. It's hard work, but it never gets boring. My coaching calls are fifteen minutes per call, so I do up to ten and a half hours on Mondays when I'm coaching."

Most people would find it hard to maintain focus for so many hours one task during one day, but Bob manages through a typically efficient strategy: "I ask each student to send me the agenda they want to go over on Saturday or Sunday. That gives me time to think about it before I talk to them."

••

It is only as we develop others that we permanently succeed.
Harvey S. Firestone, founder of the
Firestone Tire and Rubber Company

••

Doug Ferguson also finds it rewarding to coach others and he says, "If you want to coach other people it's got to be because you want to help them. If you approach it like that, then everybody grows. It's not a one-way street."

Bob believes that while helping others realize their full potential is a very rewarding reason for coaching, there is another important reason: "It keeps me on the leading edge. If you have an insatiable desire to learn, then it's one of the best ways to do that. You can learn from the best in your industry by what they do. It's a strong Lesson:

The teacher always learns more than the students

"Way back on Day Six," says Bob, "I said the teacher **always** learns the most. You always learn more than the student does because you are able to draw on a variety of experiences. I see different people facing different dilemmas every week and once I learn how they solve them I can put it into action with my other students or for myself."

··

*The best teacher is the one who suggests
rather than dogmatizes, and inspires his listener
with the wish to teach himself.*
Edward Bulwer-Lytton, 19th Century English
novelist, poet, playwright, and politician

··

As an example of how this works, Bob describes a recent experience at a seminar with his students: "We brainstormed some ideas and I came away with five actions for me to personally follow through with. As soon as I got back to work after I came home I started putting those ideas into action. For example, because we work in a big area, people always say, 'Well, how can you sell my home if you work in Brighton and I'm an hour-and-a-half away?' All of us agreed that the solution is to take our addresses off our business cards and shift our addresses to our websites. Simple!"

Bob follows this with another example: "Because we track who visits our website, when somebody visits a second time, we send them an e-mail that says, 'Are you finding everything you're looking for on our website? If I can help you, please contact me.' It's a process of building rapport and it works really well. These are simple ideas, but I learned them from my students and I immediately applied them."

Rick Ferris says that his weekly team meetings often become coaching sessions: "If I know something that will help my staff, it would be selfish not to share it, but by teaching I always understand the message better myself."

It is hard to imagine that Bob's students always meet expectations. After all, one of Bob's own Lessons is *Many times the people you do the most for appreciate it the least.* But Bob has another Lesson to account for this. "In reality they're letting themselves down if they don't do what they committed to," said Bob. "I try to keep this Lesson in mind:

You can only take people as far as they want to go, not as far you want them to go

"In fact," says Bob, "my greatest disappointment is when I can see talent in people and how far they could progress, but they don't see it themselves. Often people don't understand what they are capable of doing. Time and again people around me fall short of what they are capable of, or they are unwilling to make the commitment to get where they want to be, or where they say they want to be. They're often unwilling to back it up with the energy and effort to get there. We now have a whole new generation, the 18- to 30-year olds, who think everything should be given to them. I think they should be called the Entitled American Generation."

Bob's assistant, Regina, has had a lot of experience with the coaching process and she is very confident about what is required for success: "The first thing a new student needs is a desire to be the best he or she can be, then once the student makes the decision to be coached the fun begins! But Bob's right, you can only take people as far as they want to go. I've seen many students go well beyond their goals simply because Bob helped them realize they can go well past any limit that they put on themselves. Most students can double their income the first year just by having a coach."

Bob's stresses that coaching is not a short- term, quick-fix solution: "People who are successful still need a coach," he says, "and the more successful they are, the more they need one. Even though the air is thinner at the top and there are fewer people they can talk to, they still need guidance and direction. It's important to remember that *everybody needs somebody they can be accountable to.* They have to understand that coaching is forever as long as they are engaged in business. In fact this is my final Lesson!

Coaching is forever

Bob applies this final Lesson as much to himself as to anybody else: "I've always had mentors, or people who I could ask questions. I think they're the reason I've progressed as far and as fast as I have. Still, when you get to your 70th birthday, you'd better have gotten a hell of a lot done or you are probably not going to!"

Here is your final set of Lessons:

- **Your life's job at this level is to be a coach to others**
- **The teacher always learns more than the students**
- **You can only take people as far as they want to go, not as far you want them to go**
- **Coaching is forever**

Final Thoughts

Tasks for the Rest of Your Life:

Hopefully you have now absorbed some or all of the lessons I have learned so that you can shorten your learning curve! It is now up to you to develop a personal program that will guide you for the rest of your life. As you have applied my lessons over the last 30 days, you will have discovered that you can achieve your dreams. Now you are ready to raise your sights even further, so you need to revisit your Life Goals to set them even higher. You will also need to rewrite your Business Plan to take these revised Goals into account.

Because you have learned about ways to improve your own coaching skills, your relationship with your own mentor becomes even more important. You need to formulate an action plan to present to your mentor. Firstly, it's time to do some housekeeping. Look back through your to-do lists from the last 30 days and put a line through all the things you achieved. From this list, choose those actions that still remain crucial to your development, and write them into a new, final action plan that will clear the backlog. Once these actions are completed, you have a clean slate to begin developing your grand strategy. I expect you to be amazed at all of the things you have achieved and accomplished.

Because you are now equipped with information you need to focus your energies and achieve beyond your dreams, it is up to you to fully implement the Bohlen Program. As I have repeatedly emphasized, that will only happen if you are held Daily Accountable. You need to renegotiate with your mentor to focus your energies on the daily and weekly actions that will keep you focused.

It's also time to revise your list of rewards and non rewards. You will find that even after a few weeks of working with the Bohlen Program, your ideas of what you can achieve will have changed. Goals that you once thought were not achievable will now seem easy. Aim high!

Congratulations!

Now that you have come this far, it's time to look back over all that you have achieved during the last 30 days. You have been working with your own mentor for some time and you will know how that, along with Daily Accountability, was the most important step in your new life. Just think about how it has focused your energy. Also, you have, perhaps for the first time in your life, defined your dreams and formalized them in writing in your personal and business plan. On top of that, you have a system of rewards and non-rewards that will guarantee you stay on track. If you achieve nothing else, these steps alone will change your life.

After following the Program for only one month, there should already be a noticeable difference not only in how you feel, but also in how others see you. For example, if you have only applied one Lesson – Just Ask Questions – you will already know what a powerful tool this is and how it can change both your personal and professional relationships.

Applying the Program I have developed to your business will take longer, but if you have been conscientious and kept yourself Daily Accountable, the results should already be appearing.

Review, Revise, Review!

Remember that when you were told on Day Sixteen that constant review and revision are very important for your progress? Now that you have finished this book, don't put it aside. It is an important review tool and you need to refer back constantly as you refine your application of my Program.

It's time for a reward

On Day Seven when you first learned about significant rewards, you were asked to decide on a modest reward for completing your first task. Finishing this book is another significant milestone so you should choose a reward not only at the level you can afford but also at the level you think you deserve. If you have genuinely worked hard to perform all of the tasks set for you in this book, you should at least allow yourself a 5, but if you think you have performed well enough, why not discuss this with your mentor and choose a more significant reward?

The big rewards, of course, are yet to come. If you apply my Program carefully and consistently, they will be yours. The promise that I offered at the start of the book was: "You change the way you live and work." By now, even after only 30 days, you should know how true that is.

I said I would teach you how to put "clear and achievable goals" in place and, more importantly, I promised to show you how to monitor your progress to keep yourself on target. Remember what I said on Day One: "It's all about focus."

So, stay focused, remain Daily Accountable, work with you mentor, constantly revise your action plans and – Achieve Beyond Your Dreams!

I would love to hear about your successes.
You can reach me at Bob@andoverhomes.com.
Here's to your new found success!

–Bob Bohlen
810-772-6911

APPENDICES

PERSONAL
AND
BUSINESS PLAN

_____

Name

_____

Date

Destiny Statement

_____

_____

_____

_____

_____

_____

_____

_____

_____

_____

_____

_____

_____

_____

_____

_____

10's

1		37	
2		38	
3		39	
4		40	
5		41	
6		42	
7		43	
8		44	
9		45	
10		46	
11		47	
12		48	
13		49	
14		50	
15		51	
16		52	
17		53	
18		54	
19		55	
20		56	
21		57	
22		58	
23		59	
24		60	
25		61	
26		62	
27		63	
28		64	
29		65	
30		66	
31		67	
32		68	
33		69	
34		70	
35		71	
36		72	

25's

1		37	
2		38	
3		39	
4		40	
5		41	
6		42	
7		43	
8		44	
9		45	
10		46	
11		47	
12		48	
13		49	
14		50	
15		51	
16		52	
17		53	
18		54	
19		55	
20		56	
21		57	
22		58	
23		59	
24		60	
25		61	
26		62	
27		63	
28		64	
29		65	
30		66	
31		67	
32		68	
33		69	
34		70	
35		71	
36		72	

50's

1	
2	
3	
4	
5	
6	
7	
8	
9	
10	
11	
12	
13	
14	
15	
16	
17	
18	
19	
20	
21	
22	
23	
24	
25	
26	

100's

1	
2	
3	
4	
5	
6	
7	
8	
9	
10	
11	
12	
13	
14	
15	
16	
17	
18	
19	
20	

Specific Goals and Tasks
I want to accomplish Prior to _____

Personal:

1	
2	
3	
4	
5	
6	
7	
8	
9	
10	
11	
12	

Business:

1	
2	
3	
4	
5	
6	
7	
8	
9	
10	
11	
12	

BUDGET

PERSONAL:	per month	per year
Home Mortgage/rent	_____	_____
Utilities	_____	_____
Insurance (Health +Property)	_____	_____
Food	_____	_____
Clothing	_____	_____
Entertainment	_____	_____
Credit Card Payoff	_____	_____
Taxes	_____	_____
Travel	_____	_____
Education	_____	_____
Total	_____	_____

BUSINESS:		
Coaching	_____	_____
Rents	_____	_____
Personal Assistant	_____	_____
Marketing	_____	_____
Phone	_____	_____
Dues	_____	_____
Education (Other)	_____	_____
Auto & Insurance	_____	_____
Company Split	_____	_____
Telephone	_____	_____
Other	_____	_____
Grand Total	_____	_____

Available for Investments   _____

Projected Yield   _____

Passive Income Target   _____

Desired Passive Income/Year   ___ ___ ___ ___ ___
                               ___ ___ ___ ___ ___

Actual Passive Income   _____

Date: _____

FINANCIAL STATEMENT

Assets

Cash on Hand   _____

Stocks and Bonds   _____

Retirement Plans   _____

Real Estate Investments:

_____

_____

_____

_____

Income Real Estate   _____

    Shares   _____

    R.E.I.T.S   _____

Art   _____

Personal Property   _____

Home   _____

Auto   _____

Boat   _____

2nd Home   _____

Total Assets   _____

Liabilities

Short Term

Credit Cards   _____

Taxes Payable   _____

Loans Payables   _____

Commercial Loans _____

Credit Lines   _____

Long Term

Home   _____

Mortgage(s)   _____

Other   _____

Total Liabilities _____

Net Worth   _____

INDEPENDENCE ACCOUNT

	Year 1	Year 2	Year 3	Year 4
Amount Invested				
Stocks				
Real Estate				
Savings				
T Bills and CD's				
R.E.I.T.S.				
Retirement Plans				
Cash Flow				
Stocks				
Real Estate				
Savings				
T Bills and CD's				
R.E.I.T.S				
Retirement Plans				
Other				
Other				
Total				

Name: _____   **Top Prospect List**   **Date:** _____

Top Prospects	Phone Number	Potential GCI	Time Frame	Rank 1-10	Last Contact	Notes
1						
2						
3						
4						
5						
6						
7						
8						
9						
10						
11						
12						
13						

Top Prospects	Phone Number	Potential GCI	Time Frame	Rank 1-10	Last Contact	Notes
1						
2						
3						
4						
5						
6						
7						
8						
9						
10						
11						
12						
13						

For information on the Caliper test go to:

www.caliperonline.com

or contact:

CALIPER
506 Carnegie Center, Suite 300
P.O. Box 2050
Princeton, NJ 08543-2050
Telephone:(609) 524-1200
Customer Relations:(609) 524-1400
Fax:(609) 524-1202

DATE	S M T W T F S	**DAILY ACCOUNTABILITY RECORD**
	DAY	Name _____

PROSPECTING

Calls:
1 2 3 4 5 6 7 8 9 10 11 12 13 14 15 16 17 18 19 20 21 22 23 24 25 26 27 28 29 30 31 32 33 34 35 36
37 38 39 40 41 42 43 44 45 46 47 48 49 50 51 52 53 54 55 56 57 58 59 60 61 62 63 64 65 66 67 68
69 70 71 72 73 74 75 76 77 78 79 80 81 82 83 84 85 86 87 88 89 90 91 92 93 94 95 96 97 98 99 100

Connects:
1 2 3 4 5 6 7 8 9 10 11 12 13 14 15 16 17 18 19 20 21 22 23 24 25 26 27 28 29 30 31 32 33 34 35

SCHEDULE / ACTIVITIES

7		
8		
9		
10		
11		
12		
1		
2		
3		
4		
5		
6		
7		
8		

PRIORITIZED TASK LIST

ABC		ABC	

Summary

CALLS		CONTACTS		F/F SET	

RESULTS / OPPORTUNITIES / ISSUES

_____
_____
_____
_____
_____
_____
_____
_____
_____
_____
_____

SUMMARY RESULTS

	TODAY	WEEK	AVG PER DAY
CALLS			
CONNECTS			
FACE TO FACE'S			

	TRANSCATION SALES	COMPLETED SALES UPDATE
TODAY		
MONTH		
YEAR		

TODAY I WAS ON TRACK ___ /10.
WHAT GOT ME OFF TRACK _____

Bob's Websites

www.RBohlen.com

Bob Bohlen makes an impact on everyone he meets - his impression is everlasting. He is a man of vision who is widely known as one of the nation's finest Realtors. Find out more about his coaching program, shadow program, and strategies for successfully marketing a real estate practice.

www.BobandLillianCoaching.com

Bob Bohlen and Lillian Montalto can help you take your career to the next level and beyond. Their business and real estate coaching program help you increase your gross commission income, generate more net profit, create more free time, improve your business and management skills, and much more.